An Insider's Guide to Workplace Investigations

An Insider's Guide to Workplace Investigations

Build the Process in Your Company

Meric Craig Bloch

Copyright © 2008 by Meric Craig Bloch.

Library of Congress Control Number: 2007909847
ISBN: Hardcover 978-1-4363-1004-8
Softcover 978-1-4363-1003-1

All rights reserved. No part of this book may be reproduced or transmitted in any form or by any means, electronic or mechanical, including photocopying, recording, or by any information storage and retrieval system, without permission in writing from the copyright owner.

The views expressed in this book are those of the author. They do not necessarily represent the views of his employer or any third party.

This information in this book provides information of a business nature and is not intended to provide legal advice. Any specific issues relating to legal or regulatory compliance should be resolved with the assistance of a competent attorney.

This book was printed in the United States of America.

To order additional copies of this book, contact:
Xlibris Corporation
1-888-795-4274
www.Xlibris.com
Orders@Xlibris.com
46477

TABLE OF CONTENTS

Introduction **9**

Part I: The Business Case For Workplace Investigations 15
    A. The Management Mindset 17
    B. Selling the Value of Workplace
       Investigations to Management 21
    C. Management Legal Obligations 26
    D. Structuring the Workplace Investigations Unit 33
    E. The Investigations Manager 37
    F. The Internal Corporate Notification Process 42

Part II: Basic Concepts Of Workplace Investigations 45
    A. Focusing on Key Risk Areas 45
    B. The Significance of Workplace Fraud 47
    C. Crisis Management 51
    D. Liaison with Key Internal Departments 55
    E. The Purposes of an Investigation 57
    F. Timing of the Investigation 59
    G. Selecting the Investigation Team 60
    H. Investigation Team Members 64
    I. Judging the Success of the Investigation 67

Part III: Conducting The Workplace Investigation 69
    A. The Four Critical Steps 70
    B. Understanding the Allegation 70
    C. The Investigator's Protocol 81
    D. The Personal Interview 85
    E. Interviewing the Implicated Employee 102
    F. Detecting Insincerity 105
    G. The Interview Memo 109
    H. Interview Problems 111
    I. Collection and Review of Documents 113
    J. Management Steps 116

K. Tracking and Metrics 124
L. Executive Summaries 126
M. Business Ethics Bulletins 126
N. Reporting to the Reporter 128

Part IV: Other Investigation Issues 129
A. Operational Security 129
B. Special Concerns of Investigations 131
C. Protecting the Findings from Disclosure 140
D. Referrals to Law Enforcement 146

Conclusion 153

Appendices
A. Compliance & Ethics Issue Reporting and
   Response Policy 159
B. Sample Mission Statement 169
C. Notification Matrix for Key Internal Departments 170
D. Notification of Investigation for other
   Key Internal Departments 177
E. Colleague Referral Guidelines 178
F. Fraud Red Flags 182
G. Critical Event Reporting Policy 191
H. Guidelines for Outside Counsel 193
I. Management Notification of Investigation 198
J. Conducting Workplace Investigations 199
K. Request for Interview 224
L. Request for Subject Interview 225
M. Instructions to Witnesses 226
N. Personal Statement 228
O. Final Investigation Report 229
P. No Retaliation Memorandum 231
Q. Business Ethics Bulletin 233
R. Close-out with Reporter 235

DEDICATION

This book is dedicated to the memory of my grandfather, Lieutenant (ret.) Isidor Winter of the Police Department of the City of New York. If all companies were staffed with people like him, there would be no need for a workplace investigations process.

Fidelis ad Mortem

INTRODUCTION

"Suspect, inspect, detect, correct, and thereby protect."

After years of watching corporate scandals unfold first at Cendant, then Enron and then WorldCom, your company finds itself in the hot-seat. Maybe your outside auditors refused to certify the company's financial statements. Maybe the government began a criminal investigation into bribes your salespeople gave to officials in other countries to secure lucrative contracts. Maybe a whistleblower just announced that the company you recently acquired in a merger has been overstating its revenue for years.

Whatever the reason, the same process unfolds. Your company's stock price plummets. The CEO, CFO and/or key executives resign, take an early retirement or are forced out. The Securities and Exchange Commission launches its own investigation, and the plaintiffs' bar files class-action lawsuits everywhere. Even your long-standing customers are nervous.

As soon as the company picks itself up off the floor, its new leadership announces that the company will not tolerate any future illegal or unethical conduct. A compliance officer is appointed with blanket authority to root out improper conduct. A code of employee conduct is drafted with high-minded concepts like "mutual respect" and admonitions to be "honest, fair and trustworthy." Employees are required to take ethics training where these golden-rule concepts are explained and institutionalized. A whistleblower hotline is created, and employees are encouraged to report any of their ethical "concerns."

All of this is well and good, but what happens when someone reports an incident of actual or potential employee misconduct? Does the company respond to the report to investigate it, remedy it or learn from it? Is the responsibility to investigate the report delegated ad hoc to a human resources manager or in-house attorney to resolve in addition to their regular duties? Or was there no real thought given to the investigations function because it was just an afterthought to the code-drafting and training?

These questions are not rhetorical. The workplace investigations unit is the linkage between ethics training and company operations. But companies nonetheless measure the success of their compliance programs by the extent of their training courses, code-of-conduct distribution, and the number of employee lunchrooms with hotline-reporting posters. If the goals of the compliance function were education and publicity, this is the way to measure it. However, these should not be the true goals.

A company's employees have a duty to enhance shareholder value by either increasing revenue or reducing loss. The success of a company's compliance function, therefore, should be measured by (i) how effectively the ethics training leads to increased awareness and reporting of actual or potential misconduct issues, (ii) how effectively the reports are investigated with the objective of, among other things, identifying how business processes can be improved, (iii) thereby reducing the company's legal, financial and reputation risks.

But this better goal cannot be reached unless your company has built an effective workplace-investigations infrastructure. An infrastructure that allows an investigation to determine precisely what happened, how it happened, and who was involved. A timely process that corrects improper activities before they attract government, litigant or marketplace attention.

A robust investigations process is not about good corporate citizenship. Investigations furnish knowledge. The process of knowledge management determines what we know about our company's risks and influences how that information can be applied. This information lets a company manage risk effectively. The products of the investigative process should be a practical and personal piece of advice to executive management. The investigation goal must be to prevent future damage to the company—by using investigation findings as a form of organizational intelligence—rather than rebuilding it after the damage is done.

The economics of capitalism and private enterprise favor risk taking. But the only way to accept a risk is if that decision is an informed one. A company must maximize its business success while eliminating or reducing unacceptable legal and financial risks. Identifying and addressing those risks through investigations places the process squarely within the business' fundamental purpose.

So why doesn't every company adopt this approach? It may be that they think the company does not have the time, personnel and resources to conduct investigations in an organized manner. Executive management may think that the value of the investigation is limited to substantiating the misconduct of a single employee, and that the business leaders are already certain of his guilt. It may also be to "let sleeping dogs lie," and ignore problems that are known to exist but which are seen as too disruptive and costly to fix. It may be a lack of imagination to see the value. It may be that they are intoxicated by their own high-minded ethics message to consider anything else.

True, many companies have historically staffed corporate-security departments or hired lawyers to look into allegations of wrongdoing, but these are not business processes with a focus on corporate counseling. There is a world of difference when you use the investigation process as a way to improve business processes and as a risk-management tool than if you think small and use it only as a way to prove that a discrete act of misconduct occurred.

But there is a risk to having a robust process. Workplace investigations are not easily done well. Even the simplest variety of investigations is not for the faint-hearted. Investigations should not to be conducted by amateurs or the poorly-trained-but-well-intentioned. An investigation is looking into the conduct of employees and insiders to the company. These people have rights and expectations, and they also have varying senses of entitlement. These considerations make investigations complex.

An investigation that is incomplete or conducted improperly also places the company in a worse position than if no investigation had been conducted. It creates a legal minefield for civil claims. A poor investigation worsens the company's position if it is seen as a whitewash or a cover-up. And the failure to maintain adequate confidentiality in an investigation turns the investigation into a roadmap for the company's adversaries to use in a lawsuit. But these risks can be minimized if the process is properly constructed.

A business case—with its own value proposition—can be made for a workplace investigations unit. A properly prepared and executed investigation gives the business an advantage. Risks are identified and addressed. Dishonest employees are caught. Restitution can be attempted.

But to do this, you need to know how to embed the workplace investigations unit in your company's culture (and this applies even to those professionals in human resources and legal departments who freelance investigations) as a business process. The ultimate value of a workplace investigations unit depends on its seamless integration in the business. The smoother the practice blends into the business routine, the easier it is to sustain.

* * *

The trust of a company by its customers is one of the most important ingredients in a company's success. Central to that trust is the company's ability to police itself effectively. Another foundation of success is conducting internal investigations and imposing discipline in a manner that employees find trustworthy and consistent with its values.

This book examines management techniques and processes to create a workplace investigations unit. It is intended as a guide for building and running a successful and valuable corporate resource. Attention is also directed to establishing investigative protocols and practices that will survive the scrutiny of business leaders, affected employees, and third parties. While the exact procedures to be followed may differ based on the company, employees or alleged conduct involved, there are certain operating principles about which those requesting and conducting workplace investigations should be aware.

A word of caution, however: this book takes a no-nonsense, view of the challenges you will face when you build a workplace investigations unit in your company. This is not a theoretical work with abstract, intellectual concepts of ethics and corporate governance. Practical guidance and basic explanations are offered, as well as candid descriptions of problems, risks and opportunities.

This book doesn't deal with the nice things employees have to say about the conduct of their colleagues. Unfortunately, we must leave that to others. This book only addresses what happens when a report of actual and potential misconduct comes to your attention.

This book is more than just a how-to guide. The workplace investigations unit, when presented and structured correctly, can stand on its own merits in a company with competing priorities and demands for resources. There is no need to rely only on the ethics process and its "golden rule" messages.

This book is intended for compliance officers, their staffs, interviewers and investigators. References to "you" are intended for clarity, and the term may apply, as the context requires, to any or all of these roles.

* * *

This book advocates a robust workplace investigations unit integrated within a company's business operations. The unit's role in your company depends on your answers to a number of fundamental questions:

What do you expect the process to do in your company? Some companies are content to use the investigations process simply to document and record incidents of misconduct when they happen. They see the process as simply an adjunct to their ethics-training program where the purpose of the investigation is only to identify when that program failed on some employee-specific basis. Other companies may have higher ambitions for the process, and they may view it as another way to identify problems that present legal, financial or operational risk to the business. Executive management may wish to leverage the unit's skills and expertise.

What do you want the output of the process to do? When an investigation is completed, a report is prepared. The report will usually provide a significant amount of information about what happened and the factors that contributed to the incident. Some companies want that information tucked away in the compliance department's files and used only for that department's internal-reporting statistics. These companies want the information to be quickly forgotten lest some disgruntled employee or potential litigant find it. However, some companies may want the information for a diagnostic tool, favoring the business-improvement value over any downside risk.

Think even harder if you want the investigation report to be used to justify a disciplinary decision regarding an implicated employee. The result of the investigation will have to withstand the scrutiny of its methodology, findings and the motives of the investigator who conducted it.

How integrated within the organization will the unit be? Some companies may want the workplace investigations unit to have a pristine, above-the-fray profile that doesn't connect with any other part of the organization. Other companies may value an in-the-trenches approach that emphasizes that the workplace investigations unit is a business process within that operation.

What will your company's culture tolerate? Like it or not, the workplace investigations unit carries with it the stereotype of the "company cop" who is indifferent to the business realities of the company's employees and is looking for someone to take the blame for the wrongdoing. If your company is in a regulated industry or has a history of centralized control, the unit will likely be perceived quickly as just part of that control structure. But if your company's culture emphasizes informality, flexibility and little top-down control, you will have to work at developing a profile for the workplace investigations unit that will avoid estranging it from the mainstream of your company.

What are your business leaders looking for? The investigation process requires the allocation of resources and executive-level support. Do your ambitions for the unit align with those of executive management? Don't rely only on their sense of their legal obligations and fears of Sarbanes-Oxley non-compliance. Too many compliance professionals already rely on the "well, they have to do this" factor rather than sell the business value of what they do.

Who are your investigators? This is both a management as well as a training issue. Are your investigators all members of the workplace investigations unit or are they professionals in other departments who will be adding investigations to their current responsibilities?

PART I

The Business Case For Workplace Investigations

For some companies, the workplace investigations unit is built around preparing for the day when the company receives a catastrophic misconduct allegation, such as the apocryphal whistleblower reporting that she saw the CFO shredding financial documents. That is, frankly, a poor allocation of company resources. If such a situation happens, the company's response will take on a life of its own regardless of how much advance thinking tried to plan for it. If the situation happens a second time, the company may not survive regardless of how the investigation is managed.

The practical reality is that the vast majority of misconduct is of a lower level. It is transactional. It is small mistakes. But each of these matters, especially when they can be repeated in similar situations elsewhere in the company, quietly bleeds the company one drop at a time.

Because of its proximity to the compliance function, consider the relationship of the workplace investigations unit to ethics. Business ethics is, to a large extent, a measurement of good and bad conduct as a company defines it. For most companies, the ethics process is generally represented by their code of conduct, their formal ethics training, and the employee-discipline process. The workplace investigations unit is one of the tools of the ethics process. It examines improper behavior and informs management of the facts pertaining to the incident.

The success of the workplace investigations unit depends, in great part, on the profile of the compliance program in your company. Compliance programs are not profit centers of a business. Consequently, there must be some rationale for funding your program. If your company funds a compliance program simply out of fear of prosecution or because your competitors have these programs, the future of the workplace investigations unit is precarious because the group's survival depends on factors outside its control. Similarly, if the program exists without concrete expectations and metrics to measure its business value, then the unit is also at risk.

Investigators must remember that we are not in the morals business. We are in the investigations and prevention business. But we need to do more, or we will be relegated to the corporate equivalent of the people who follow the elephants in the parade with brooms and shovels. There is plenty for us to do.

> **Process Pointer:** Devote some thought to the improbable goal of putting yourself out of business in your company. It will never happen, but it is a worthy goal. If you have such ideas as goals, it is more likely that you will get closer to that goal than if you do not.

You must, if for no reason other than self-preservation, recognize your obligation to contribute to the equity value of the business—increasing the returns to its shareholding owners—and this must be a fundamental operating principle. But your believing is not enough. Your executive management is going to have to be convinced that you are not just another layer of bureaucracy to be endured.

Start by changing their perceptions.

What Do We Mean by an "Investigation?"

Any discussion of an investigations process depends first on a definition of an investigation. An investigation is the systematic and thorough examination into something and the recording of that examination in a report. In the corporate context, the primary purpose of an investigation falls within one of these categories:

- Thoroughly documenting incidents of misconduct in order to maintain a permanent record of their occurrence.
- Identifying the root cause of an incident where improper conduct is suspected.
- Identifying people involved in misconduct.
- Compiling information that proves or disproves an allegation or that implicates or exonerates someone suspected of misconduct. This is especially true if the investigation is used to justify disciplinary or similar post-investigation action.

Who are the Customers of an Investigation?

It is useful to use the term "customer" in referring to those who experience the investigations process firsthand. Some people may voluntarily seek the assistance of the workplace investigations unit, such as colleagues in Human Resources or executive management—to investigate a specific allegation. These customers want help with a specific problem and seek a specialist to help them accomplish something. But often a "customer" is engaged involuntarily by the process, such as an implicated employee, reluctant witness, or a manager who would prefer to wish the problem away. Furthermore, a "customer" always includes the executive managers who rely on the investigation's findings to improve business processes.

A. The Management Mindset

Accept the possibility that your company views a robust workplace investigations unit as a want, not a need. Effective compliance programs are a good thing, your management will no doubt acknowledge. But how will you convince your company to devote resources to your effort to build an investigations infrastructure if the only incentive offered is a chance to be seen as a better corporate citizen? Increased attention to the workplace investigations unit will be seen as a smart investment only if the company perceives it as adding value.

You must market the specific value of the investigative unit. If not, investigations will be just the company's ad hoc response to a complaint. Because executive managers are among the "customers" of an investigation's outcome, it pays to know how these senior managers generally view business issues.

> **Process Pointer:** You risk your job security if your unit is seen just as some corporate fad. A number of years ago, the "diversity" fad swept through corporate America. Few recall it having any true business relevance. Where is it now?

Being in Control

Business people generally like to be in control. For example, a regular business practice is to define a goal, formulate a strategy, and execute a plan. By controlling the outcome as much as possible, managers can ensure the most profitable result. This is what they are paid to do. Not surprisingly, the managers value the profit motive more than almost any other factor.

This mindset will influence a company's perception of the workplace investigations unit. Managers will want to know what commitment must be made to complete an investigation. But until the facts are known, required commitments for an investigation can only be estimated. Senior business managers may want the ability to conduct workplace investigations with their own resources or within their own business units because the managers believe they can control the outcome. Successfully leverage that mindset by developing the investigations process to provide a reasonable assurance to these managers that the outcomes will serve the business interests of the company and its shareholders.

> **Process Pointer:** Knowledge about business risks and threats, and then making informed business decisions, is true control.

Threats to Employee Loyalty

Managers may be reluctant to embrace the investigative process because they may believe it jeopardizes employee loyalty. Call it the "witch hunt" factor. Loyalty is critical to worker productivity, efficient operations and good customer service. Loyalty also reflects the extent to which employees trust their employer and believe that the employer is truly interested in their well-being. Employees are unlikely to remain committed to an employer they do not trust. While most employees would not suggest that fellow employees who committed some misconduct should be protected from discipline, the efforts of a third party—in this case, your investigators—may be seen a threat to this loyalty bond. Unless marketed well, efforts to engage management will not overcome the preconception that you are conducting an inquisition and looking for someone to take the blame.

The Role of Incentives

Business people, especially sales people, focus on the rewards they get in their jobs. They tend to screen out any distractions—including compliance messages—which interfere with achieving those rewards. So if your sales team is rewarded with commissions and bonuses, they are probably going to focus only on what is likely to achieve that commission or bonus.

No legitimate business openly encourages its employees to break the law. And that business would not exploit the vulnerabilities of its employees to achieve the same end. But it is nonetheless possible for incentives operating behind the scenes to have the same effect.

Identify what motivates your sales force and the messages they get from their managers. Do not underestimate or misunderstand these forces.

> **Process Pointer:** Never forget what motivates business people and the rewards and punishments they receive in their jobs. Abstract concerns like "we could be sued" or "we want to be ethical" cannot compete with the pressures to achieve this quarter's sales goals. If you want their support, you must speak their language and appeal to what they consider important.

Over-Reliance on Policies

Business people are not oblivious to problems in the workplace. However, most companies tend to respond to problems like misconduct with some quick solution and then move on to the next "fire" to be extinguished. For example, drafting and implementing business policies are a good way of managing the legal and practical issues that arise in a company's transaction and operational life. Policies codify best practices and attempt to ensure consistency and quality. But policies are not quick-fix solutions that can be applied like a Band-Aid to legislate a problem away. The short attention span for most executives works against a big-picture perspective on a problem. The company rarely takes the time learn whether the policy solved the problem as a useful business tool or whether it became an inconvenient restriction that hindered the business and was quickly ignored.

Additionally, creating just another corporate policy as a way of managing the business risk only addresses the symptom. It makes the business leaders feel productive, but it does not address the underlying source of the problems.

> **Process Pointer:** An over-reliance on corporate policies is disingenuous. If not for the investigation process, how will your company determine whether these policies are effective or just window-dressing?
>
> The fault for simplistic compliance-related messages is ours, not the fault of the business leaders. In many companies, we chose to present ourselves as the "morality police" because it was both easy to do so and flattering.

Practical Business Realities

Business leaders generally don't see the tangible benefits of investigations. This is often due to the fact that the usual investigation scope and the findings are not made relevant to the world in which they operate. Consider the realities which exist in their world:

First reality: Business people are hired—and fired—depending on their ability to generate income for the company. Compliance programs are not profit centers of a business. So unless you have something to say that has a bottom-line significance, they probably won't care too much.

Second reality: The lack of involvement of business managers in structuring compliance programs in general has caused much confusion about the proper role of ethics in business. There are many ethical "gray areas" in business dealings. However, ethics is often presented—usually by those who do not work within a company department with profit-and-loss responsibility—as a kind of moral absolutism. The examples in ethics training are often presented in a simplistic way, as if every real-life situation has a right and wrong answer (such as "should I lie, cheat or steal"). With its emphasis on "doing the right thing," managers believe that you are simply asserting the obvious, so managers do not take the message seriously.

Third reality: Managers generally believe that investigations are neither profitable nor expeditious. Business people know that the profitable use of time is the key to their success, and the investigation may seem more expensive than simply writing off the loss, firing the offending employee and going back to the business of selling goods and services.

Fourth reality: Workplace investigations are usually not tied to the operation of the business. The goals were usually to identify wrongdoers and then calculate the harm they caused. The business people already assumed that Bob stole the money, so what does the investigation do for them?

Fifth reality: Companies are starting to question Sarbanes-Oxley requirements and their costs. Foreign companies are delisting from domestic stock exchanges or offering IPO's abroad. Enron is old news. Dangling concepts like the Thompson Memorandum and the Sentencing Guidelines will not persuade executives in most companies.

Sixth reality: People who work in companies over time learn that, every few years, some new corporate fad pops up, and then everyone is supposed to pay homage to it. Relying on abstract messages about ethics and compliance will over time leave the workplace investigations unit as just another layer of bureaucracy that gets conveniently ignored, only to be mentioned in superficial newsletters and lunchroom posters.

Increased attention to compliance and investigations will be considered a smart investment for your company's leadership only if they though that the risks of noncompliance were tangible. Otherwise, added compliance will be seen as little more than an insurance policy—with its own share of overhead costs—for something that is not likely to happen.

B. Selling the Value of Workplace Investigations to Management

Before you can sell the business leaders on an improved approach to investigations, you will need to have a good professional relationship with them. There are many ways to build good relationships with senior managers. Some of them include:

- Respect their legitimate business objectives and redefine your success to include the achievement of those objectives.
- Respect their limited resources by delivering value and properly managing their expectations.
- Respect their decisions to take calculated risks in running the business.
- Respect the fact that you are assisting the executives to run their business, and they are entitled to direct the battle plan.
- Build trust with senior executives. This influences your credibility and determines whether your message is convincing or not.

There are also some key selling points to use in soliciting the support of the executive management.

Return on Investment

Like other business functions, the workplace investigations unit should have a measurable return on investment ("**ROI**"). A properly engineered investigation produces tangible results, such as the recovery of money, the termination of dishonest employees, and prosecution of wrongdoers. The more substantive the ROI, the more likely the process will be embraced by the company and receive the funding it deserves.

Traditionally, investigations return value to the company by

- Stopping financial losses.
- Changing processes and procedures to improve operations.
- Increasing productivity.
- Obtaining restitution or concessions from wrongdoers.

The financial impact of a successful investigation is important to recognize. For example, if your company's EBITDA (earnings before interest, taxes, depreciation and amortization) is ten percent, your company has to generate $10 in revenue for every dollar it pays out in losses. Conversely, every dollar recovered through a successful investigation equals $10 in revenue your company did not have to generate.

> **Process Pointer:** EBITDA—that's speaking their language. Develop a payout example using your company's financial data to show the value you bring (as well as the cost for doing nothing).

Risk Management

Running a business is all about taking smart risks and calculated risks. But not all risks are created equal. Proper risk management includes the ability to recognize potential hot spots. This leads to better decision making regarding how much risk the company wants to reduce, transfer or avoid. It allows executive management to manage problems when they are still small and relatively inexpensive to deal with. Investigations are valuable components of a company's efforts to identify systematically the risks to the business and to ensure that appropriate processes commensurate with the risks are implemented.

Although they focus on specific allegations against past conduct, investigations actually provide some foresight. If the investigation findings are seriously considered and gleaned for "lessons learned," the findings will offer insights into how similar problems may be occurring elsewhere and in the future.

In risk-management terms, investigations identify existing sources of revenue loss and preventing further losses. Investigations shield the company from liability or help reduce it. Your company may become aware of problems or practices which could expose the company to criminal liability, civil lawsuits or sanctions. Identifying and repairing these problems before a possible outside investigation begins can give the company the opportunity to take remedial measures, comply with relevant laws or regulatory standards, or eliminate other problems that were previously unknown to management. Finally, aggregate workplace-investigation data can be presented to show risk trends of certain employee behaviors, troubled management, or business regions.

> **Process Pointer:** Most misconduct is the result of a combination of factors: an opportunistic person enabled by poor business practices. This is why risk identification is an important part of any investigation. Don't rush to conclude that the misconduct happened in a factual vacuum.

When seen this way, investigations avoid future costs. When conducted in-house, the transactional cost of an investigation is minimal. They offer value to business because they connect investigations with financial and operational policies and procedures. Timely and meaningful findings avoid damage to reputation and investor confidence. They protect the stock price. They avoid the personal liability of directors and officers. They avoid civil litigation and criminal penalties. On a practical level, a thorough investigation may even help the dispute-resolution process of company claims by identifying the strengths and weaknesses of your company's position.

Ask yourself how to calculate the value-added of a properly conducted investigation when senior executives consider these questions:

- How much could be lost if the risk is not managed intelligently?
- What is the company's vulnerability to the risk?
- Is the risk correlated with other risk exposures?

- If some think the risk is minimal, how can we get assurance that the confidence is justified?
- How much will it cost to manage the risk?
- Is there a potential reputation risk impact from the risk?

In a perfect corporate world, executive management partners with you to identify and prioritize business risks. This gives the executive management a stake in your unit and maximizes the value of investigations to the business.

Proper risk management gives the company some competitive benefits:

- Improved ability to prevent, quickly detect, correct, and escalate critical risk issues.
- Reduced burden on business operations.
- Reduced costs by improved sharing of information and integration of risk-management functions.
- Improved strategic flexibility for both upside and downside scenarios.
- The ability to provide a comfort level to the board of directors and executive management that the full range of risks is understood and managed.

Good marketing makes the investigation process an essential part of that value proposition.

Good Corporate Citizenship

Companies want to be perceived publicly as good corporate citizens. Corporations generally want to be recognized in the relevant community as a contributor to shared values through the creation of jobs, income to the community and the payment of taxes. To the extent that the corporation can build a constituency beyond the shareholders, the greater the likelihood that company senior managers will see the benefits of an effective workplace investigations unit. But don't forget that, unless tied in with business-oriented goals, this public-service message will be ignored as just another appeal to a business senior manager's conscience, with predictable results.

> **Process Pointer:** Never presume that you care more about the company than your colleagues in other departments. It is likely that their efforts, rather than yours, drive the revenue into the company that pays everyone's salaries. Also, the "moral high ground" is an off-putting message. Be careful with the ethics messages. These messages should be used only to complement the business case for the process.

Projecting a Strong Public Image

Attention to ethics is good public relations. The fact that a company regularly gives attention to its ethics portrays a strong positive to the public. People see those companies as valuing people more than profit, as striving to operate with the utmost of integrity and honor. Aligning behavior with values is critical to effective marketing and public relations programs.

Stakeholder Expectations

Investigations which identify misconduct serve your company's broader interests by helping the company meet the expectations of the business' internal and external stakeholders. (A stakeholder could be the company's employees, shareholders, government agencies or outside groups.) A business that incorporates ethical principles into its operations will likely fare better in the market. If an ethical lapse then occurs in the future, the risk of adverse publicity will be less as the public may see it as an aberration in the company's otherwise clean image.

Quality Control

Properly conducted investigations are a form of organizational intelligence, provided that the focus is not limited to the simple question of whether misconduct actually occurred. Information gleaned from an investigation improves business operations by identifying deficiencies in operations. When done well, investigations offer executive management each of the following:

- Company values, ethics and expected behaviors are communicated to employees through the conduct of the investigation and the application of a code of conduct.
- Key business risks are identified and assessed.

- Information can be reported to management, the board and stakeholders in an accurate, timely and reliable way.
- The company's true culture can be measured, as well as the need for additional training or better management supervision.

> **Process Pointer:** Experience is the best teacher. You can expect that an incident that has occurred will occur again if the underlying causes have not been corrected.

The Tip of the Iceberg Concern

It seems reasonable to believe that most employees report only a fraction of their concerns and allegations to the attention of the compliance department. As a result, complaints of possible or actual misconduct must be taken seriously.

Each complaint is important in its own right. Each complaint may also reflect similar concerns held, but unexpressed, by other people. Companies should take all the feedback they can get as opportunities to learn how processes may work more effectively and efficiently.

Business Counseling

Your investigation findings need not only speak for themselves. Offer your value to the business. Become fully integrated into the functioning of your company (or the business divisions you serve). Become an active participant in meetings and ask questions. This enables you to appreciate the issues that the company facts and get to know the political dynamics without your company. The better you understand the business leaders, the better you can advise them. The more you can advise them, the more valuable you and the unit will be perceived.

C. Management Legal Obligations

Fortunately for you, the company's decision to investigate misconduct is not just a voluntary business decision. Certain legal principles underscore the need for management to investigate reports of actual or potential misconduct.

The Duty to Investigate

In most situations, the decision to conduct a workplace investigation is left to the discretion of the company. Whether the amount of the suspected loss or the wrongdoing involved is sufficiently serious to warrant an investigation is a business decision that depends on considerations of costs, time and other resources. Also, the likely return on investment is considered.

There are circumstances, however, when the company has no practical alternative but to begin an investigation. That duty may arise from statutes or regulations, contracts with customers and employees, and even a common-law duty to properly supervise employees.

Legally speaking, a company's management and board of directors have a fiduciary duty to act in good faith with the care of an ordinarily prudent person when managing the company's affairs. This general standard requires directors, officers and other fiduciaries to use the same reasonable care in conducting the business of a company that they would in their own affairs, and always to put the interests of the company ahead of their personal interests. Accordingly, the duty to investigate arises under normal fiduciary duties. If the company is a public corporation, directors also have a duty under the federal securities laws to investigate when information comes to their attention indicating that the company's management may have engaged in fraud, or that the company's prior public statements may be inaccurate.

Legal and regulatory duties to disclose misconduct outweigh a desire by executive management to ignore an employee or managerial offense. The best way to fulfill these legal duties and requirements is simply to investigate known or suspected misconduct.

This may seem like an obvious point: why wouldn't an employer want to investigate possible misconduct? Wouldn't an employee want to conduct an investigation so that it could remedy the problem, stop its losses and prevent future problems? Consider that an investigation may have adverse consequences. When your company admits publicly that it is a victim of employee misconduct, it may harm the company's image. The admission can expose the company to civil or criminal liability. It can affect the stock price. The investigation may unintentionally provide its competitors and adversaries with previously unknown information that can be used against the company.

> **Process Pointer:** Don't overestimate the duty to investigate misconduct. Just because a company has to investigate does not determine how they have to do it. The company can still perform a bare-bones investigation if it wanted to.

Vicarious Liability for Employee Misconduct

Under some circumstances, an investigation may help the company avoid criminal or civil liability for an employee's misconduct. An employer is generally liable for any misconduct committed by an employee within the course and scope of his employment. "Within the course and scope" means that the employee performed acts of the kind he was authorized to perform and that the acts were intended, at least in part, to benefit the company. The fact that particular conduct was wrongful does not necessarily mean it was outside the course and scope of employment. As a result, the company may be held liable for the illegal acts of its employees.

However, if the company has clearly established policies and standards prohibiting employees from engaging in the particular kinds of conduct, and if the company shows that it regularly enforces those policies and standards by meaningfully investigating the reports it receives, a court may conclude that the employee's conduct was not within the course and scope of employment, and the company would then not be liable. Enforcement of policies and standards requires, among other things, that management thoroughly investigate alleged violations whenever they occur and that they enforce the policies through appropriate discipline to wrongdoers.

Sarbanes-Oxley

The Sarbanes-Oxley Act of 2002 forever changed corporate governance in the United States. The law and other recent developments reflect an acceleration of the trend towards requiring corporations to adopt effective compliance programs and initiate workplace investigations to deal with allegations of misconduct. The law created new criminal penalties and increases the scope and severity of old ones. For example, Section 406 of the Act requires disclosure of whether the public company has adopted a code of ethics for senior financial officers, and if not, why not. Section 404 requires that a public company's annual reports include a discussion of the existence and effectiveness of internal control structures. (Investigations are considered to be a form of internal control structure.)

Sarbanes-Oxley imposes a number of measures designed to enhance corporate honesty and accountability. Some of its provisions require audit committees to establish procedures (such as a hotline) for receiving and dealing with complaints and anonymous employee tips regarding irregularities in the company's accounting methods, compliance controls, or auditing matters.

Sarbanes-Oxley requires a company to investigate whistleblower complaints quickly and competently. Otherwise, this might be considered a lack of "compliance controls" under Sections 302 and 404 of the Act. If the company rejects any whistleblower claims, the company must be prepared to explain a competent basis for its assessment and rejection of the claim.

Sarbanes-Oxley also makes it illegal to retaliate against whistleblowers. Companies must therefore ensure that reporting employees remain protected. Any employee who reasonably believes he was retaliated against because he reasonably believed that fraud was occurring has a civil cause of action against the company. The law also makes it a federal crime to retaliate against a whistleblower that has assisted law enforcement.

Management, with good reason, pays close attention to the application of Sarbanes-Oxley rules to its financial documents, financial reporting documents and public statements. They know that the market will punish any irregularities or discrepancies that are reported publicly. Auditors also assess a company's compliance financial controls. A good investigation does precisely the same thing: evaluate and assess the company's business operations to minimize risk and ensure appropriate business conduct. (By making these linkages, you leverage the impact of Sarbanes Oxley and then benefit from the attention management pays to its requirements.)

> **Process Pointer:** Don't hide behind SOX and similar laws. As time passes, no one is afraid of them as much as they once were. Companies are pushing back. Some foreign companies have delisted from US stock exchanges. Even the SEC is getting pressure to pare back some of the requirements.

Possible Federal Prosecution

There will be times when misconduct could not be or was not detected by a workplace investigation. In some cases, your company may find itself exposed to criminal liability. The United States Department of Justice has issued a set of guidelines which gives a significant inventive to embed the investigations function in compliance programs in its memorandum on the "Principles of Federal Prosecution of Business Organizations." This memorandum is named after its author Deputy Attorney General Larry Thompson, and it is known generally as the "Thompson Memorandum." The Department of Justice placed new emphasis on the role that a company's cooperation would play in the prosecutors decision to bring charges or to negotiate a plea agreement.

The Thompson Memorandum specifies nine factors for federal prosecutors to consider. Three of these factors relate to an effective corporate compliance program:

4. the corporation's timely and voluntary disclosure of wrongdoing and its willingness to cooperate in the investigation of its agents, including, if necessary, the waiver of corporate attorney-client and work product protection;
5. the existence and adequacy of the corporation's compliance program;
6. the corporation's remedial actions, including any efforts to implement an effective corporate compliance program or to improve an existing one, to replace responsible management, to discipline or terminate wrongdoers, to pay restitution, and to cooperate with the relevant government agencies . . . .

The Thompson Memorandum explains that "the critical factors in evaluating any program are whether the program is adequately designed for maximum effectiveness in preventing and detecting wrongdoing by employees and whether corporate management is enforcing the program or is tacitly encouraging or pressuring employees to engage in misconduct to achieve business objectives." The ultimate goal is to "determine whether a corporation's compliance program is merely a 'paper program' or whether it was designed and implemented in an effective manner."

The mere existence of a compliance program will not relieve a corporation of criminal liability. The Thompson Memorandum warns that criminal conduct "in the face of a compliance program may suggest that corporate management is not adequately enforcing its program." Properly conducted investigations, as part of a well-designed and effective compliance program, may meaningfully reduce the risks of a corporate prosecution by federal officials.

Organizational Sentencing Guidelines

The United States Sentencing Commission's Guidelines for the Sentencing of Organizations have become increasingly strict, thereby raising a company's exposure. The Guidelines combat white-collar crime by imposing mandatory sentences, harsh fines, imprisonment, restitution and public disclosures through imprisonment. The Guidelines work in tandem with the provisions applicable to individuals to cover the broad range of offenses with which federal prosecutors can charge corporate defendants.

Even where company liability cannot be avoided, it may be mitigated by efforts that include an effective investigation of the misconduct that caused the liability. Under the original Guidelines, federal courts use a prescribed formula to determine fines for organizations that have committed (or are vicariously liable for) felonies. Fines under the Guidelines are based on two factors: the seriousness of the offense and the company's level of culpability. The seriousness of the offense determines the base fine. The company's culpability is a measure of the actions taken by the organization which either mitigated or aggravated the situation.

Four aggravating factors that *increase* the culpability score and, therefore, could increase the penalty imposed are: (i) the company's involvement in or toleration of the criminal activity; (ii) the company's prior history of wrongdoing; (iii) whether an existing court order was violated; and (iv) whether there was obstruction of justice.

In 2004, the Guidelines were amended to make the criteria more rigorous with the intention of making boards of directors and senior managers more accountable for the oversight and implementation of a compliance program. Requirements were added to require a company to promote a culture of compliance within the corporation. The amended Guidelines provide two mitigating factors that *reduce* this culpability score and, therefore, could decrease the penalty imposed. These two factors are (i) the existence of an effective compliance and ethics program; and (ii) the company's efforts to self-report, cooperate with authorities, and accept responsibility.

An "effective program to prevent and detect violations of law" means a compliance program that has been reasonably designed, implemented and enforced so that it generally will be effective in preventing and detecting criminal conduct. The seven components that a company must show include:

- Standards, including a Code of Conduct.
- An active role played by the company's board, executive management and ethics officer.

- Due diligence in hiring and promoting law-abiding personnel.
- Training and other forms of communications.
- Audits and evaluations of the program, and a hotline.
- Discipline for violations.
- Remedial actions when a violation is discovered.

Failure to prevent or detect the offense, by itself, does not mean that your company's compliance program was not effective. An effective program to prevent and detect violations of law is one in which the company exercised due diligence in seeking to prevent and detect the criminal conduct.

Accordingly, if a company accepts complaints through a hotline but takes no further action to investigate or remedy the situation reported, this may result in liability. Not acting on the call puts the company at risk under the Guidelines. Offering an anonymous reporting mechanism but not acting on calls into question the effectiveness of the compliance program.

As a general matter, the Guidelines' description of an effective ethics and compliance program has become an industry benchmark for assessing corporate compliance practices.

Unit Legitimacy

These persuasion points are necessary because senior management tends to have little understanding of the investigations function, perceives it as not being proactive, and does not see it as contributing much to business decisions. If you have successfully advocated for your workplace investigations unit, base that conclusion on each of the following elements that are necessary for success:

- Unrestricted access to your company's leadership.
- The ability to influence strategic business decisions.
- The unit is an acknowledged stakeholder in your company's risk-management process.
- Executive management supports the unit's goals and responds appropriately.
- Sufficient resources are allocated to the workplace investigations unit.
- The unit has a positive effect on your company's ethical health.
- The unit has exclusive ownership of the investigations process.

D. Structuring the Workplace Investigations Unit

So you managed to convince your company's executives to support your grand plan to investigate misconduct. The next challenge is how to construct the workplace investigations unit. The investigative function must be tailored to your company's specific needs, depending on your company's history, industry, and key business risks.

Tailoring the Process

There is no "one size fits all" investigations process. Your company must develop a process which its leaders believe will best prevent and detect violations within the organization. Several factors should determine the contours of the process:

- *Size of the organization*—How formal and elaborate a process depends on the size, complexity and culture of your company. The industry in which your company competes is another consideration.
- *The likelihood that certain types of misconduct may occur because of the nature of the company's business*—When there is a substantial risk that certain types of violations may occur, the company's management must develop a process that meaningfully detects and prevents those types of offenses.
- *The company's history*—This factor considers the types of offenses the company should have taken steps to prevent in the past. Preventing the recurrence of known problems should be foremost in the minds of executives trying to make the investigations process effective and relevant to the company.

> **Process Pointer:** Some companies establish or restructure their investigations process in response to a particular corporate scandal the company just survived. While past history should guide you, do not rely on it exclusively. The process should not be simply reactive to a specific event, and it should be proactive enough to have a strategic purpose for the company's future. This will ensure the long-term viability of your function.

Funding the Process

The principal resources of an investigations function are people, information, physical assets and financial assets. The determination of the primary focus of the function dictates how the function is structured and how resources are allocated. The amount of resources the company is willing to dedicate to the function determines how many investigators can be hired, what technology and equipment can be acquired, even how high a corporate profile can be maintained by the workplace investigations unit.

Investigation funding is challenging because needs are often difficult to project. One complex investigation, especially if it requires the engagement of outside experts, can skew the budget projection—or overrun—for a particular year.

One of the best ways to help fund the process adequately is to show value to the company or demonstrate that the process pays for itself. You may strengthen your budget justifications with any of the following:

- Focusing investigative goals on the company's strategic and business needs.
- Tracking historical investigations costs accurately.
- Implementing cost-effective strategies.
- Pursuing restitution and recovery where possible.
- Quantitative estimation of risk avoidance.

Formal Corporate Policy

You want something from your company's board of directors or executive management to give you the necessary corporate authority to establish your process. The policy document serves as a statement from your company's leadership that the company affirmatively mandates the investigative process and that primary responsibility for this function is placed with you. A sample corporate policy may be found in Appendix A.

The statement gives the workplace investigations unit credibility and authority in the company. A good policy also addresses the functional needs of the unit. The policy should make your unit responsible for the reporting to the company leadership of all misconduct-related matters. Even if matters are handled by other departments, all upward reporting should be done through your unit. The workplace investigations unit should be the single voice on this subject.

Second, employees should be obligated to report matters of suspected or actual misconduct as part of their job responsibilities. Some companies give employees a number of places to report the incident, and others direct the employee to their whistleblower line. (The use of the whistleblower line is valuable when an employee wants to report misconduct but wishes to remain anonymous.) There must be some mandate to speak up, or the workplace investigations unit risks not knowing about something that might be going on.

Third, your department must conduct the investigations of any non-routine matters. Key internal departments like Human Resources can continue to handle the garden-variety matters they usually do.

Fourth, your department should be empowered to specify both the investigations process for the company and the investigation protocol to be followed. This will create the benchmark for the company. Deviations from the standard are permissible as a particular investigation requires, but these articulated standards at least ensure that the deviation was the result of an informed decision.

Fifth, the policy should specify periodic reporting obligations. There should be reports submitted monthly or quarterly so the leadership can measure the company's ethical health. (It will also let you continually showcase the value of the workplace investigations unit to the company.)

The corporate policy will specify the basic structure of the function. But regardless of its precise contours, there are still certain considerations common to any company's investigation process:

- What misconduct will trigger an internal investigation?
- To whom should the incident or misconduct be reported?
- When should an investigation begin?
- Who should conduct the investigation and how should it be conducted?
- What should be the purposes of the investigation?
- What types of disclosures outside of the workplace investigations unit are necessary?

> **Process Pointer:** If you can't get a board-of-directors mandate, why bother having a robust process? You then care more about the risks to the business than they do. You cannot survive without the board as your advocates.

Your workplace investigations unit may want to create its own Mission Statement to define—and clarify—its role in your company. A sample corporate policy may be found in Appendix B.

Independence

You cannot even appear to be influenced by management. The independence of the workplace investigations unit ensures that the results are a fair determination of the facts learned. The company should consider placing the responsibility in an independent department that is not part of a business unit within the company. Interference, whether regarding timing, methods, witnesses to contact, which documents deserve heightened scrutiny or ultimate determinations reached destroys the credibility of the investigation process. The workplace investigations unit will be seen as an inquisition, a management tool, or just irrelevant to the business. It will also increase the risk of liability to the company.

Consistency

Responses to allegations must be consistent and predictable. Employees must believe that a response to misconduct will be handled the same regardless of the implicated person's management level.

Navigating the Political Winds

A workplace investigation takes place within a matrix of competing business interests. Inside the company, the boards of directors, the audit committee, management, employees and shareholders often have different goals and perceptions of their interest. Players do not always put the company's interests above their own. Outside the company, competitors, the press, the company's auditors, the market, and the government all have varying motives and concerns.

One of the most important things you can do is convince upper management—and the board of directors if necessary—of the importance of understanding and solving the problem under investigation. This is crucial to obtaining adequate resources and authority for the investigation and to obtain proper credit for helping the company deal with the problem.

E. The Investigations Manager

Traditionally, investigations were conducted by members of the legal or human resources department. There is now a trend toward more autonomy, professionalism and objectivity in the management of this process. There are some clear advantages for the use of an independent workplace investigations manager to oversee the investigation process.

The Corporate Counselor

The Investigations Manager supervises the overall investigations process and the workplace investigations unit. The manager is responsible for keeping the process working and the investigation objectives in focus.

The Investigations Manager has more than just a procedural role. The manager must have the skills to translate the value of the investigation process and findings into forms of risk management and business counseling. The manager must have nontraditional compliance competencies such as business partnership, industry knowledge, communications skills and teaching. Business expertise and financial skills enhance the manager's value further.

Because investigating possible misconduct and its related business failures involve questioning someone's judgment and putting a stop to activities that may be both popular and lucrative, the Investigations Manager needs sufficient tact and clout to carry out the function. Similarly, because company policies will be investigated, the manager should have experience both in the company generally and as a manager to be credible to those who may be investigated or to whom the findings are reported.

However, some will claim that the appointment of an Investigations Manager undermines the goal of encouraging corporate colleagues to work together amicably by threatening the cohesion that binds them. This view is correct only if investigations are conducted poorly. A properly conducted investigation—which includes an appreciation for your company's political forces at work—reassures management that the investigated deficiencies or errors are viewed in a realistic, marketplace context rather than a perfect world. The fact that the Investigations Manager must continue to work with these people, cultivate them as allies and customers of the investigative process, and encourage them to refer future matters actually makes it more likely that the Investigations Manager will be able to navigate internal operating forces successfully.

The investigative process is not an exact science. So the Investigations Manager must be sufficiently experienced and creative to represent the interests of the workplace investigations unit to executive management. This requires good skills in "corporate diplomacy," especially when important executives would prefer a quick disposition to a matter that, in the best interests of your company, requires a more thorough examination.

The Investigations Manager needs to be more than an able defender of the process. The manager must also be open to an informal and open exchange of ideas with colleagues in other departments. Some investigations may need to be tailored—again, in the best interests of the company—to minimize disruptions to operations or to accommodate some unrelated business need. The Investigations Manager has to find some way to bring together the sum total of these competing interests and still ensure a proper investigative result.

The Process Controller

An Investigations Manager specializes in investigations and should have significantly more experience than either the company's in-house attorneys or the human resources managers. These other professionals often, however experienced in their own disciplines, normally handle misconduct investigations as only as a small part of their traditional responsibilities. The investigations they conduct are also likely to suffer from their competing time priorities. A full-time Investigations Manager also shows that your company does not have a "part-time" approach to investigating workplace misconduct.

The Investigations Manager acts as the final authority and the solely responsible individual for the conduct of the investigation. The Investigations Manager must believe that the results of each investigation support the conclusions as to the type of the management decisions that are available, that are supported by the findings, and that can bring the matter to a conclusion.

A good Investigations Manager also understands the nature of litigation because that's where many investigations lead. The manager understands the concepts of evidence, discovery and the other issues related to litigation. As an employee, the Investigations Manager understands the workplace and business operations better than an outside counsel retained to conduct the investigation. The manager also understands the company's culture and the internal company politics that may expedite, or impede, corrective action. The effective Investigations Manager uses his or her knowledge of the workplace to help draw out the facts of the case. The manager will be better known to company management and its employees. This may result in more effective persuasion of company management that action is necessary and better cooperation in requests for information and interviews.

The Case Manager

Case management means the internal procedures for collecting, recording, organizing and preserving all the various pieces of information gathered in an investigation. This is your company's official record of the matter. If there is a lawsuit, regulatory action or prosecution, these are the key materials that will be reviewed to determine if your company's actions were proper or if your company may pursue a claim affirmatively.

Case management is necessary in all types of investigation. Proper management begins when the report is first received. It continues until the investigation is closed and the findings are reported.

The Investigations Manager is singularly responsible for case management. This includes each of the following duties:

- Ensuring that proper notes are taken, whether of interviews or physical examinations.
- Preparing, or causing the preparation of, official reports that document the investigator's activities.
- Maintaining separate case folders for each investigation that contain all the reports, documents, and other information relating to the investigation.

Case management keeps track of what has been done and what needs to be done in an investigation. Proper documentation and updating allows all interested parties to understand the basis for any later company action. If the investigation extends over a long period of time, proper case management allows the investigator to refresh his or her memory and to identify any facts that remain to be developed.

Using Technology in Case Management

Most companies use computer software to track investigations and develop analytics of investigative trends. If your company chooses a technology platform for case management, the Investigations Manager should be responsible for maintaining the investigations database.

A case management platform allows for easy case assignment and workload management. It facilitates the need to monitor progress of an investigation, assign specific tasks and keep investigators from becoming overloaded. Specifically, a good platform allows the Investigations Manager to ensure each of these:

- Document each report received of actual or possible misconduct.
- Confirm that appropriate authorizations are in place and internal notifications have been made to begin the investigation.
- The progress of each investigation is timely and adequately reported.
- Financial issues such as asset values and estimated losses are recorded.
- Investigation objectives are tracked and updated.
- Case resources are managed.
- Post-investigation information is recorded.

The Investigations Manager as Trainer

Teaching investigative skills (especially to part-time investigators in other departments) and specifying your company's investigations protocol are vital responsibilities of the investigations Manager. Training should be conducted in a variety of ways to suit the existing skills and experience levels of the investigators. A good way to train investigators, for example, is to assign the novice to work with a more-experienced investigator. Like many disciplines, classroom instruction in workplace investigations is only of limited value. It must be combined with controlled, practical experience to be a valuable learning tool.

The Investigations Manager establishes guidelines in advance to avoid allegations that the company proceeded on an inconsistent or capricious basis and will minimize the time and effort spent addressing procedural issues when the need for an investigation becomes apparent. The guidelines should cover when an investigation will be conducted and how the investigation will proceed. The guidelines may also cover who determines the need for an investigation and who will oversee it. Specific guidelines also ensure the integrity and confidentiality of an investigation.

The Coach to the Investigators

The Investigations Manager must also be the motivating force to the investigators. To them, the Investigations Manager is the face of upper management. The manager is their advocate and protector when the going gets rough. This is not a trivial point. There are a number of issues that investigators face, and each of these affect their attitudes and ability to close a successful investigation:

- Being required to defend your findings in court, to regulators and second-guessing executive management.
- Spending extensive time and effort on an investigation that is later shown to be based on false allegations, reports or information.
- Investigations may not be resolved, terminated without resolution or may result in what the investigator believes is an inappropriate disposition.
- Some investigation may stretch out for an extended period, leaving the investigator to feel that they are not making sufficient progress.
- Investigators may be subject to ethical temptations.
- Witnesses and corporate colleagues may be uncooperative or frustrating.
- Executive management may not share the investigators sense of urgency or decide that an identified problem is not as serious as they do.
- The reluctance of law enforcement officials or prosecutors to accept a case after significant effort has been expended.
- Investigators may become cynical and pessimistic about the integrity of their colleagues.

An Investigations Manager is not required to be a psychologist to be effective. However, being alert to these signs will ensure an efficient and effective workplace investigations unit.

> **Process Pointer:** Think of the Investigations Manager as part quarterback, traffic cop and big brother to the process. As to senior management, the Investigations Manager should be seen as equal parts "reality therapist" and "organizational pathologist."

F. The Internal Corporate Notification Process

If the workplace investigations unit is going to be useful to your company, you must ensure that you learn of these incidents when they arise. The need is most clearly identified with incident management. For example, most companies have a plan specifying roles and responsibilities once executive management learns of a serious incident that threatens the company. This presents the second hurdle to overcome. Incident-management plans are often generic documents admonishing employees to report a list of vaguely defined events to their superiors when they occur. This "silo" approach may accomplish the upward reporting of incidents, but such a plan does not ensure cross-department notification of incidents.

At the other end of the spectrum, it isn't much better. Don't just rely on your hotline. Most of those calls are of the "I hate my boss" variety. Referrals from other key internal departments are your best sources for matters to investigate. A model matrix may be found in Appendix C. A template memorandum to notify other key internal departments that you received a report whose subject matter affects their part of the business may be found in Appendix D.

The notification matrix has a simple goal: the notification to and inclusion of key internal departments in the resolution of a specific incident category. The matrix does not determine which department leads the resolution of the problem, but it ensures that each department with a stake in its resolution will be included. (In reality, because each incident will have unique facts and varying internal concerns, it is not helpful to define responsibilities in advance. Proper discussion internally will often divide responsibilities easily.) Including these internal departments facilitates the resolution by making that department's substantive skills available to the investigation.

The first step in preparing the matrix is to define those categories of risk your company faces. Your company's code of conduct is a good first step. Then the company should also identify (i) what level of risk exposure requires immediate action; (ii) what level of risk requires a formal response strategy to mitigate the potentially material impact; and (iii) what events have occurred in the past, and at what level were they managed?

Your goal should be a workable document that can be reasonably understood throughout the company. Use plain English and common-sense definitions. Don't worry about including every factual variation of an incident that falls within the category. Be extra careful if the matrix will be distributed internationally and used by non-native English speakers.

Don't forget that company bookshelves are filled with formalistic "thou shalt" policies. Coupled with the fact that most employees want to do the right thing but are not always sure what the right thing is, there is no reason not to craft a matrix that gives practical guidance. It is a meaningless exercise if it will not be accepted and integrated into your company's operations.

The second step is to identify your company's key internal departments. For most companies, the legal, human resources and finance departments are obvious choices. Be sure to include specific business units because they are a key reporting source of incidents. This will also create some loyalty with those units because most incidents will affect the revenue stream from an impacted customer, and the matrix provides for their involvement. Consider, if appropriate for your company, other departments such as corporate security, internal audit, or public relations.

The third step, of course, is to determine which departments will be notified for a specific incident category. The compliance office should always be notified. Once the assignments are done, executive management should formally approve the matrix and agree to abide by it.

Early knowledge about misconduct-related incidents often eludes compliance departments, especially in larger companies. Do not discount the fact that the matrix will also assist the necessary efforts to ensure effective reporting to the group of actual or suspected misconduct. Adhering to the matrix, therefore, enhances the quality and quantity of the information you will collect and report to executive management.

Because the goal is to actually learn of incidents, do not just rely on the matrix. Give practical instructions to the people who usually inform you. These practical instructions can be basic referral guidelines to let them know about what, when and how to inform you. These guidelines should mirror the basic structure of the matrix because it is a continuation of the same process. Sample guidelines may be found in Appendix E.

Mitigating the risks of foreseeable incidents with an effective investigative process should be critical for any company. It takes a concerted and ongoing effort to integrate the workplace investigations function with the functions of other internal departments to make an effective incident management program. Properly done, you have one more opportunity to demonstrate the value of their groups and to embed them further within the company's operations.

> **Process Pointer:** A good notification process is essential to the survival of your process. Otherwise, how can you have any confidence that you will be informed when incidents occur? And even with the process, don't forget your diplomacy and salesmanship skills to cultivate these key internal colleagues.

PART II

Basic Concepts Of Workplace Investigations

The workplace investigations unit will not investigate every possible issue the company faces. Your investigations generally will be limited to specific areas, so your process must also respect the operating boundaries of your sister departments in the company.

A. Focusing on Key Risk Areas

Workplace investigations traditionally focus on allegations of employee misconduct. The difference among companies often depends on how the company defines "misconduct." If the company has a detailed code of conduct—and if the investigations function is linked to ethics training—then workplace investigations tend to follow the scope of the code of conduct.

Most codes of conduct are substantively identical. Misconduct under these codes generally falls within one of these categories:

- Accounting Irregularities
- Antitrust and other Competitive Issues
- Conflicts of Interest
- Confidential Information
- Employment Practices
- Fraud
- Insider Trading and Information
- Internal Business Operations
- Internal Workplace Conduct
- International Trade Controls

- Kickbacks and Bribery
- Misuse of Internal Company Systems
- Money Laundering
- Political Activities
- Records Retention
- Regulatory Noncompliance
- Retaliation against Whistleblowers
- Substance Abuse

The need for an investigation, however, does not arise simply because the code of conduct was violated. The business value of the workplace investigations unit is more than simply serving as an adjunct to the ethics process. The investigations function could be expanded to cover issues with any of these characteristics (even if they fall outside the code of conduct):

- Deliberate or reckless attempts to circumvent normal business procedures or controls.
- Violations of Sarbanes-Oxley or any other law or regulation concerning corporate governance and oversight.
- Systemic or pervasive concerted action directed toward a group of people.
- Any involvement by a corporate officer or a member of the board of directors.
- Potential material financial impact to a business unit or the company.
- Likely potential harm to the company's reputation or a risk of adverse publicity.
- Likely potential for a significant lawsuit against the company.

An investigation should be conducted when the nature of an allegation requires some level of detailed fact-finding, rather than simply dealing with the employee-specific matters. The fact-finding could be needed to identify a business-process breakdown, the extent to which training or management oversight is needed, and the possibility that the misconduct may be repeated elsewhere in the company. Effective fact-finding also facilitates dispute resolution when management learns of all the "bad facts" and possible contributory fault by others.

> **Process Pointer:** Do your own risk analysis. Consider those areas where your company is vulnerable. What business risks are peculiar to your industry or market?

B. The Significance of Workplace Fraud

Your company, like other companies, will specify misconduct categories in a way that works for its particular circumstances. This classification process helps because, among other things, it allows the presentation and analysis of aggregate data. If the categories are too sweeping for example, serious incidents will be combined with garden-variety ones, leading executive management and outside auditors to misunderstand problems in the company. But to the workplace investigations unit, classification data is secondary.

The reality of workplace investigations is that most misconduct falls into one of two areas: personal misconduct and fraud. Some may criticize this as an oversimplification, but the truth is that fraud accounts for the vast majority of financial misconduct in a company. Personal misconduct is, of course, a most relevant area for investigation. But the threat to the company of personal misconduct, especially when the Human Resources department traditionally addresses this area in conjunction with the workplace investigations unit, is usually much less than the financial and reputation risks of fraud.

Fraud detection and investigation should be among the primary responsibilities for your workplace investigations unit. Even if that responsibility is shared with other key internal departments, your unit must be the leader in investigating allegations of workplace fraud. Whatever competence your peers have in their own disciplines—legal, internal audit or human resources—the reality is that the workplace investigations unit may be the only qualified internal source for a proper investigation. Accordingly, the workplace investigations unit must have at least a basic knowledge of fraud as it relates to the corporate context.

Reports of fraud will come from a variety of sources: an allegation from a third party, an investigator's suspicion, an auditor's discovery or the discovery that something—cash, reports, files, etc.—is missing.

Workplace fraud can be committed by company insiders (executives, managers, employees and agents) or by outsiders (vendors, contractors, or suppliers). The workplace investigations unit should be concerned mostly with fraud committed by insiders, as that will compose the majority of reports.

Workplace fraud can also be classified according to whether the insiders committed the fraud against the company (such as theft, corruption and embezzlement) and fraud to assist the company (such as violation of government regulations, improper public disclosures, etc.).

Fraud is a Human Phenomenon

The scope of this book limits a discussion of the myriad of factors and characteristics of workplace fraud. But there is room for one salient point: fraud is a human phenomenon.

Fraud is both personal and environmental. An employee who commits fraud could be motivated by greed or some economic need. The motivation could be a need to preserve his or her status in the company. The company's culture—such as win at all costs, the ends justify the means, etc.—can both encourage and facilitate fraud in the company.

Frauds committed by executive management involve the misrepresentation of facts in financial statements. There could be an overstatement of assets, or an understatement of expenses and liabilities. The fraud could be committed to deceive lenders and investors by inflating profits. The rewards could be higher salaries, bonuses or stock options. The reward could also be as basic as the desire to keep your job.

Frauds committed by lower-level employees will be, fortunately for your company, more numerous but less threatening to your company's survival. These frauds include expense-account padding, embezzlement, using company property for personal reasons, accepting payments from company vendors and suppliers. Transaction-oriented frauds can occur in any variety of ways, and these will differ based on your particular industry.

What is fraud?

Fraud is a broad legal concept that generally refers to an intentional act committed to secure an unfair or unlawful gain. It covers the following categories of risk that can undermine public trust and damage a company's reputation for integrity:

- Fraudulent financial reporting (e.g., improper revenue recognition, overstatement of assets, understatement of liabilities).

- Misappropriation of assets (e.g., embezzlement, payroll fraud, external theft, procurement fraud, royalty fraud, counterfeiting).
- Revenue or assets gained by fraudulent or illegal acts (e.g., over-billing customers, deceptive sales practices, accelerated revenue, bogus revenue).
- Expenses or liabilities avoided by fraudulent or illegal acts (e.g., tax fraud, wage and hour abuses, falsifying compliance data provided to regulators).
- Expenses or liabilities incurred for fraudulent or illegal acts (e.g., commercial or public bribery, kickbacks).

Who commits fraud?

Many people who commit fraud are first-time offenders. The Association of Certified Fraud Examiners found that only 12 percent of those people had a previous conviction for a fraud-related offense. In addition, fraud is most often committed by employees who hold executive positions, have been with a company for a long time, and who are respected and trusted employees.

Anatomy of a fraud

Knowing how to investigate fraud requires one to know how and why fraud occurs. Fraud investigators often refer to the "fraud triangle," which illustrates the three necessary components of fraud. Without all three components, fraud will not occur.

The first part of fraud is opportunity. There must be some vulnerability in the system for a fraud to occur. That vulnerability may be something as simple as poor security. Often the opportunity is trust. Management places trust in an employee and therefore gives that person access to assets and systems, and that access creates the opportunity for fraud.

The second part of the fraud triangle is motive. Motive is the reason behind the fraud. It is often some sort of need, whether real or perceived. A real need may be paying for an expensive medication or paying the electric bill. A perceived need is something that the perpetrator wrongly believes she or he needs, such as a luxury car or extra spending money.

Motives may also include a need for revenge against a company or person. Balancing perceived inequities can also be a powerful motive, such as in the case of a person who feels unfairly compensated when compared to his peers. Motives include any sort of trigger that may cause an employee to decide that fraud is the answer to the problem.

The third part of the fraud triangle is rationalization. In order to commit fraud, the person has to justify to himself that it is permissible to do the act. For some, this may be easy, as dishonesty may be a way of life. For others, rationalizing theft is a little more difficult. Perpetrators of fraud may tell themselves that they need the money more than the company, that they are simply righting a wrong, or that the company deserves to be defrauded because of lax controls.

Perhaps the most important lesson to be learned from the fraud triangle is that normally all three factors must be present for fraud to occur. If any one of the three elements is missing, fraud will normally not occur.

Simply punishing people who are caught committing fraud is not an effective way to deter fraud. There are several reasons why this is so:

- Employees who commit fraud only commit their crimes when there is a perceived opportunity to solve their problems in secret. In other words, fraudsters do not anticipate getting caught. The threat of sanctions does not carry significant weight with the employee because he never expects to face them.
- Employees who commit fraud rationalize their conduct so that it seems legal or justified. Thus, they do not see their actions as something that is or should be sanctioned.
- Because employees who commit fraud are primarily motivated by status, the greatest threat they face is that their crime will be detected. Detection will result in loss of status. Any sanctions that follow are only a secondary consideration.

> **Process Pointer:** Be your company's fraud experts because real dollars are involved and you can make a difference. Also, fraud concepts are counterintuitive and will not generally be understood by your colleagues in Internal Audit and Human Resources. Corner the market with your unique knowledge.

Fraud Red Flags

Even though fraud is concealed, sooner or later a fraud can be detected. Rarely will something expose the entire fraud scheme at once. Instead, some detail—a fraud indicator—will catch someone's attention. These indicators are called the "red flags" of fraud.

A list of common red flags may be found in Appendix F. The presence of red flags does not mean that fraud has occurred. Instead, it means that the company should ensure that some investigation is done to determine whether the company should be concerned. Red flags are not a substitute to the proper factual predicates that justify beginning an investigation in your company.

The workplace investigations unit has the opportunity to be the company's fraud experts. When corporate realities require every internal department to demonstrate its relevance to the company's bottom line, this is an opportunity that you can afford to miss. Even if another department detects the fraud, position yourselves as the resource to investigate it.

> **Process Pointer:** Workplace fraud occurs millions of times a day. Most of it is trivial and petty, but it can be cumulatively expensive for your company. Focus the efforts of your workplace investigations unit on the more egregious kinds of workplace fraud—intentional schemes by dishonest employees to loot the company of its assets.

C. Crisis Management

There will come a time when some unforeseen event will arise that the company will consider a crisis. Whatever the type of crisis, the defining characteristics will include a dynamic, fluid situation where decisions have to be made quickly, often based on imperfect information. There is a role here for the workplace investigations unit because, in most companies, the investigators are the company's premier fact-finders. Don't miss the opportunity to integrate the unit into your company's crisis-management plan.

Reactive crisis management is management responding to an event that threatens the operations or success of the business. Crisis management in the face of a current, real crisis includes identifying the real nature of a current crisis, intervening to minimize damage to the business, and recovering from the event.

Many companies try to be proactive and draft internal protocols to respond to unplanned incidents, seeking an integrated business process approach that considers the entire enterprise. These plans recognize that a coordinated response and sharing information among key internal departments like compliance, legal, finance, human resources and public relations is critical. A sample Critical Event Reporting Policy may be found in Appendix G.

The risk to the company in not having an crisis-management plan is not just that local managers will resolve an incident at their level without alerting executive management. It is also only some of the internal departments with a stake in the incident's outcome may not be included in the resolution process. Among other things, the company then loses the benefit of the missing department's expertise.

The basic elements of a crisis are always similar: (i) the occurrence of a surprise harmful event; (ii) a loss of control; (iii) a lack of reliable real-time information available to decision makers; and (iv) a siege by people harmed by the event and the media covering the event. The senior executive must take control of and assume responsibility for the crisis situation, define the problem, deploy available resources promptly, efficiently and effectively and bring the crisis under control.

So don't be left out. Look at your company's crisis-management process for an opportunity to enhance the value of the workplace investigations unit. Even where a company has already formulated its crisis-management plan, consider expanding your charter beyond just investigating and recording occurrences of actual or possible misconduct.

Your investigation can offer practical and personal advice to executive management during a crisis. You can seize the opportunity to partner with their business peers and become executive management's "first responders" when an incident occurs. This will give further support for a compliance group is essential role as an embedded business function within the operations of the company.

So what exactly is Crisis Management?

Some estimate that every major company faces a significant incident every three years. Most companies, however, are not well suited to a coordinated response, and they do not have the structural features to encourage a collaborative approach. Company operations tend to be fragmented and decentralized. There is often little central visibility and oversight. Efforts and technologies are often duplicated among unrelated departments. Experiences and "lessons learned" are rarely shared.

While any incident can cause corporate harm, companies which develop an crisis-management plan believe that an incident can less harmful to the company if you see it coming. "Crisis management," therefore, means the process by which a company recognizes events (or a combination of events) that materially threatens the business, reacts appropriately to those events, and then responds to quickly resume normal corporate operations. The "crisis" means any unexpected, negative event involving potential damage to the company's stakeholders, processes, technology, infrastructure, brand or intangible property. Events range from internal and external security breaches, significant theft or internal fraud, unintended privacy violations, to unexpected financial situations.

Remember that "unexpected" does not mean unforeseeable or just disastrous. The incident management approach anticipates that the incidents arise with regularity and predictability in the lifecycle of the company. This is another reason why the compliance professionals are well-situated because their risk-management role encompasses identifying foreseeable risks and anticipating their potential occurrences.

How does the workplace investigations unit get a role?

An effective crisis-management plan should, but usually does not, depend on the participation of the workplace investigations unit. Other corporate departments, such as legal or public relations, may have seemed to plan drafters as obvious team members. But consider that many crisis-management plans focus on two factors: (i) what departments should be included in the plan, and (ii) how should they be alerted. These plans, while looking good on paper, likely miss the scarcest commodity when a crisis occurs: information. Every important decision—dealing with employees, handling the media, anticipating a lawsuit either defensively or offensively—depends on knowing precisely what happened and what is continuing to happen. This is not to say that the people within management have no information about the incident, but it is more likely that no one decision-maker has all the information reasonably available on which to base important decisions.

Therein lies your opportunity. First, crisis response teams are often built with an enterprise-wide, cross-discipline perspective. Because your group likely covers the entire enterprise and report directly to the CEO or the Board of Directors, this positions them outside a particular business group.

Second, you have the skills to conduct the type of detailed investigation that the incident requires. This cannot usually be said for your corporate peers

The Investigators' Value

Any serious incident poses some important questions to senior managers. Is the primary objective of the company's response to remediate the problem? Is it to communicate and report the incident? Is it to marshal the company's resources and information to prosecute someone?

The upshot of this is that when an incident occurs, the first challenge is usually to learn all the knowable facts, accurately, completely and with minimal risk to the company's legal position. The impact of the incident must be quantified and prioritized. Executive management cannot be unnecessarily diverted from their regular corporate duties. Liability issues must be evaluated.

Managed properly, the investigation can give some structure to the company's handling of the crisis. In his bestselling book *Winning*, Jack Welch offers five assumptions for executive management to keep in mind when a crisis happens. Each one can be adapted to the workplace investigations process as part of incident management:

"**Assumption 1: The problem is worse than it appears**." Investigators usually do not restrict the scope of their inquiries to the known facts or the perceived misconduct. Frequently, as an investigation proceeds, the scope will widen or narrow depending on the facts developed. In a crisis, management may try to downplay perceived bad facts or not be forthcoming with investigators. Because of their independence within the company, investigators will not feel the pressure their corporate peers may feel to minimize the problem or shade the facts.

"**Assumption 2: There are no secrets in the world, and everyone will eventually find out everything**." Seasoned investigators conduct investigations with the assumption that any part of the investigation may be disclosed publicly. They do this work professionally. Investigators know that the possibility always exists that the facts elicited, the sources of the facts, and the investigation process itself will be subject to later scrutiny by third parties and adversaries.

"**Assumption 3: You and your organization's handling of the crisis will be portrayed in the worst possible light**." The time for using the best investigative resources available is when a crisis occurs. The investigation must be conducted as professionally and thoroughly as possible. Even so, some will likely accuse the investigators of "white-washing" the matter under investigation. Others will complain that the company is being too aggressive in the investigation and is on a "witch hunt." Yet another reason to go to the company's strongest investigative resource.

"**Assumption 4: There will be changes in processes and people. Almost no crisis ends without blood on the floor.**" If the investigation focuses on determining the true facts concerning the affected business processes and people, then you provide genuine value to the company. In a crisis, accurate facts may be hard to determine, especially under time and management pressures. Executive management may be looking to dismiss those they believe are responsible in order to repair the company's public image. The investigation provides these decision-makers with objective facts about what precisely happened and how it occurred.

"**Assumption 5: The organization will survive, ultimately stronger for what happened.**" The crisis and the facts determined from the investigation can provide a number of lessons to the company, if the company has the courage to confront what happened. There can be no lessons learned unless the investigation was conducted properly.

(Welch, *Winning* [Harper Business 2005], pp. 153-161.)

> **Process Pointer:** Consider how to make misfortune an opportunity for your workplace investigations unit. When a crisis happens, this is your golden opportunity to showcase your skills to company at a time when the focus of the company's leadership is on you.

D. Liaison with Key Internal Departments

One of the best ways to maximize the effectiveness of the workplace investigations unit is through liaison with the key internal departments in your company. Liaison could be formal or informal, individual or departmental. Liaison allows the workplace investigations unit to leverage the resources of others, share best practices and collaborate on specific cases. Issues of common concern—for example, working with Human Resources in a misconduct investigation—can be addressed with the sharing of information and resources.

Encourage your investigators to develop their own network of contacts in your company. Professional relationships with law enforcement agencies and with peers in other companies (such as through trade associations) should also be encouraged.

Effective relationships facilitate effective investigations. The other departments also become your allies, advocates and part of your "early warning system" for detecting threats to the business which must be investigated.

Who to Contact

Consider an introductory visit and periodic follow-up visits with key people in the company. Exchange information and favors. Your list of internal contacts should include the following people, at a minimum:

- Your chief executive officer and his staff
- Your chief financial officer and his staff
- General Counsel
- Contracting or procurement officer
- Human Resources director
- Public Relations officer (or equivalent)
- Information Technology manager

Liaison in Multinational Companies

If your company is multinational, liaison relationships become even more critical. The intricacies of culture, local laws, privacy policies, language differences and local familiarity. Local contacts can assist in the investigation and help investigators keep a low profile.

International liaison contacts should be developed before a crisis or investigation begins. When traveling for other business reasons, make some time to develop your contacts and become familiar with the issues your team is likely to face if a later investigation becomes necessary.

How to Maintain Liaison

Once established, liaison relationships need maintenance. After all, even the most proper professional relationship is also based on mutual need. Consider the following suggestions:

- Make sure you and your counterpart derive some benefit from the relationship. Even if there is not an exact quid pro quo, the relationship must be mutual.

- Follow proper limits on gifts and other expressions of appreciation.
- Never violate the trust of a liaison contact. Protecting reputations—yours and theirs—should always be paramount.
- Maintain periodic contact, even if there is no specific information to exchange. This will remind your contact that the relationship remains important.
- Don't forget that, in many relationships, you may need them more than they need you. Their function may be a true fixture in the corporate landscape—CFO and Human Resources are two good examples—and yours may not be. Good salesmanship and diplomacy skills should always be used.

The existence of organizational issues that the workplace investigations unit shares with other internal departments can actually work to the unit's advantage. At first glance, it would appear that these other departments are competitors for scarce resources. But sharing the issues actually makes you partners in the same goals.

> **Process Pointer:** If things were perfect in corporate organizations, there would be no need to partner. But things are not perfect. Partnerships, like marriages, carry an element of risk as well as reward. Be judicious in limiting the amount of risk in integrating your goals with those of the other internal departments.

E. The Purposes of an Investigation

The investigations process has its own business objectives. An understanding of these purposes helps embed the workplace investigations unit in your company. Investigators are no different than any other company employee; their job is to serve some business purpose designed to enhance shareholder value.

Meaningful Objectives

No investigation of any complexity can be successful unless specific objectives are determined in advance. The objectives of the investigation decide the investigation's starting point and where it is intended to finish. The objectives determine the fact-finder's purpose, measure his progress, and provide the framework by which the Investigations Manager builds the case for post-investigation handling.

Properly articulated objectives also protect the company. They lay a defensive foundation against possible claims later on that the investigation was improperly motivated, a "witch hunt" or a rambling inquisition against imagined wrongdoing with no beginning or end. The company is protected when it can be demonstrated that, from the beginning, the intentions and objectives of the investigation were legitimate, professional and proper.

Determining the Facts

In most companies, the fact-gathering process to investigate a misconduct allegation is handled primarily as a personnel-management matter. There is often little or no focus on professional fact gathering in methods that tend to assure the credibility of the evidence. In the absence of a professional process, one that can be examined to determine the equity of the process and outcomes, the accuracy of the fact-gathering—other than as a way to justify terminating employment—remains a shortcoming in many companies.

The context in which your investigation is conducted must be to answer the most basic question: what happened. The investigative process determines the facts, establishes the facts which are sufficient to cause a reasonable person to recognize that the facts are or are not what they are reported to be.

In a misconduct investigation, the accusations must be credible, relevant and truthful to bring the level of proof to a standard where management should be expected to determine responsibility. The investigation also determines whether any other people were involved besides the implicated person. By identifying the subject's modus operandi if misconduct is proven, you will highlight gaps in internal controls.

Establishing Accountability

An investigation establishes accountability as to how an event happened and what mitigating circumstances may exist that affected the outcome of the event. The investigation does not critique management style, unless specific management actions contributed to the circumstances which permitted the event being investigated to occur.

Maximizing the Decision Process

Investigators are in the business of information gathering. Information developed from an investigation maximizes options for those managers who must decide on the solution. The only way management decision-makers can be offered the maximum number of options is if the investigation is done right.

F. Timing of the Investigation

Investigations vary in complexity and the length of time to complete them. However, all investigations must be conducted promptly. A timely investigation gives the company more time to develop appropriate responses or defenses.

Timeliness is part of a professional investigation. Timeliness is important for other reasons as well:

- Innocent people should be cleared as soon as possible.
- Corrective action is generally more effective when taken closer to the triggering event.
- Ongoing misconduct must be stopped as quickly as possible.
- Morale may suffer in the investigated department while waiting for the outcome.
- Delays create the perception that these reports are not important.
- Over time, it becomes more difficult to obtain accurate statements (and some employees may leave the company).
- The investigation will assist in any legal action that may arise in connection with underlying matters.
- Promptness may be a mitigating factor in almost every level if government enforcement, and delay or indifference can be seen as an aggravating factor.

Whether a particular investigation is timely depends, of course, on that investigation. You will generally set the timetable that gives a reasonable amount of time to conduct the investigation. You must ensure its timely completion.

That being said, no investigation should be completed too quickly if that expedience means that the quality of the resolution will suffer. You may have to resist pressure from outside sources—pressure that may be either reasonable or otherwise—to either rush or stall a case. As with many things, balancing competing interests is the key.

G. Selecting the Investigation Team

Choosing the wrong people to conduct your investigation guarantees a poor result. The right investigator, however, depends on the particular facts of the case. Don't assume that the same person can proficiently conduct every type of investigation. The right investigators understand the business, have credibility with the executive management and are seen as impartial with no vested interest in the outcome of their investigation.

The investigator is the fact-finder. In some cases, the investigator simply makes the findings. In other cases, the investigator may fulfill the role of fact-finder, business counselor and dispute resolver.

The challenge in assembling the investigation team is the need to develop in the team an investigative mentality. An effective workplace investigations unit shares some important qualities.

Relevance

This quality is listed first because it is probably the most important. All the other qualities are immaterial if the investigation is not made relevant to the needs of the business.

Every risk in a business is a business risk. At some point, as an issue moves up the corporate structure, it becomes a business risk. A legal risk becomes a business risk at some point. A flaw in operations, a financial fraud, the misconduct of an important manager all become business risks.

This means that whatever the facts are that prompted to the investigation, the investigation's output must be directed to how the business can benefit from the findings.

On a practical level, proper considerations of relevance will also ensure an efficient investigation because it keeps the investigation's scope limited only to the necessary issues.

Proper Mindset

Doubt is one of the primary attributes of any investigator. You should remain appropriately skeptical. Do not assume that management or employees are honest and telling the whole truth until the facts are gathered and the inquiries are complete. Have sufficient imagination to develop sufficient theories against which to compare factual evidence as it develops. Persevere until the anomalies are resolved and the fact pattern is thoroughly understood. Finally, have patience to find the smallest detail that less-experienced people may overlook but that can provide that vital clue or inconsistency. You will discover the truth as a result of your ability to inquire and learn from that inquiry.

Professionalism

The essence of professionalism is that you conduct the investigation with integrity, fairness and diligence. How the investigation is conducted reflects the professionalism of the company. Often the integrity of an investigation is judged by the reputation of the investigator. You must be sufficiently senior to communicate and/or implement investigation plans. You must also be able to maintain the confidentiality of sensitive information.

Similarly, you must be fair and even-handed. If the employees believe that the investigations process applies to lower-level workers but somehow exempts the senior managers, the workplace investigations unit will not survive.

Independence

You must be free from actual or apparent bias or conflict of interest. Consideration must be given to whether an investigator's judgment may be affected or criticized by previous biases or political considerations, whether real or not. For example, an in-house investigator should not investigate the conduct of his or her superiors. Also, investigators who witnessed the underlying conduct cannot participate in the investigation.

Independence means that everyone gets a fair chance, and that each implicated person is investigated in the same manner, with the same professional, impartial, objective treatment.

Competence

The quality of an investigation also depends on your competence. You must have the skills that are matched to the type and nature of the investigation you are handling.

The ability to investigate and interview effectively is an acquired skill. You must have the experience and the expertise to conduct a credible investigation. You must understand how to interview witnesses, manage documents and other records, and to maintain any applicable privileges to the extent possible. You should also be fully informed about company policies, procedures and company history. You must know the management controls and strategies employed by the relevant business unit. You must be able to contribute to the discussion of risks to the business, highlighting the potential likelihood or severity of risk areas.

Competence also includes the quality of accuracy. The investigators must be able to effectively collect and sort data from a variety of sources, human and otherwise. Each investigator must be qualified and able to observe and accurately record data. The findings will depend on these skills.

Objectivity

Throughout our lives, we develop our own set of values. These values influence the way we live and the decisions we make. These values are subjective. They are shaped in part by gender, by education, by race, by intellectual capacity, and by personal experience. But these have nothing to do with the reported conduct in an investigation which must be viewed objectively. All information must be reviewed and analyzed using the same standards, and the findings in an investigation should be based on the facts, not an opinion filtered through your personal value system. Understand and factor in your own natural biases.

Avoid even the appearance of bias or conflict of interest. This depends to some degree on the seriousness of the matter. Even when the company has its own investigators, some matters may be so sensitive, and the scope so broad, that outside counsel become the appropriate choice to conduct the investigation. You must also determine whether the nature of the allegations or the identities of any potential wrongdoers might prevent you from conducting a thorough investigation.

You can demonstrate your objectivity in two effective ways. First, you can decide not to participate in deciding the investigation's objectives. This might show that you had no particular interest in its outcome and, similarly, no personal agenda to pursue. Second, you can exclude yourself from the decision-making process at the end of the investigation. By not being party to the decisions regarding corrective action, such as employee discipline, you have no part in the outcome. Because you have no interest in the investigation's objectives and outcome, it would be difficult to accuse you of bias or prejudice in your findings.

> **Process Pointer:** Doubt does not equal cynicism or an assumption that everyone is lying. Doubt means that you refuse to assume things are true without proof, and you always keep your mind open for other explanations.

Objectivity also does not mean jumping to conclusions without first independently corroborating the facts. The goal should be to allow the facts developed through the investigation to speak for themselves.

The investigators must also project an air of objectivity. This can be done by choosing their words carefully during interviews and by avoiding body language that might project an inappropriate attitude.

Fairness

Fairness is important, but it means different things to different people. But fairness to the people under investigation shows that you are a true professional.

Fairness means being truthful to witnesses. When an implicated person asks what proof exists against him, fairness means telling him the truth. It is not exaggerating the quality or quantity of the proof. It is not telling him that everyone thinks he is guilty when, in fact, only you believe that. Being fair simply means you are being honest. It is being professional with both actions and words.

Thoroughness

A good investigator will follow all relevant leads to their logical conclusion and focus on corroborating key findings. This means checking all leads and double-checking others. Some leads may appear to be of secondary importance, and the investigators must make decisions regularly to strike the balance between efficiency and thoroughness. Pressures like time and resource constraints as well as the disruptive effects of investigations must always be balanced against the need for a thorough examination of the facts.

H. Investigation Team Members

The Investigations Manager determines the appropriate investigator for a specific investigation. If necessary, the manager should work in conjunction with internal audit, human resources or risk management if an investigation requires their assistance. The manager also retains private investigators, outside counsel, and certified fraud examiners as needed. Staffing the investigation requires a consideration of the advantages and risks of appointing certain personnel as investigators.

Lawyers as Investigators

Lawyers are generally thought to be best-suited to investigate because investigations typically involve interviews with company personnel (some of whom may be hostile), the analysis of complex facts, and a final determination as to whether there have been any civil or criminal investigations. Most lawyers are experienced at examining witnesses, sifting through facts, and ranking both in order of their importance. Certainly, experienced attorneys are able to determine the necessary obligations of the company in each particular circumstance, and counsel will make recommendations concerning what actions to take as a result of the investigation.

However, lawyers do not usually make the best investigators. Although they are skilled in gathering evidence and preparing a case, their expertise is generally limited to some area of the law. Also, many lawyers never met a legal issue they didn't like. They can leave no stone unturned in analyzing an issue while losing sight of the big picture—the client's overall business needs.

Lawyers also may not have the skills needed to advise the company on whether and how to continue to conduct its business operations differently in the future. Lawyers are predisposed towards assessing risk rather than proposing a business-focused resolution. It would be unusual that they could serve in the other roles as a business counselor, trouble shooter and operations improver. Learning about "bad facts" in an investigation is a tool to be used to improve the business, not a risk to be avoided lest the company get sued by someone who finds out about it.

There are also certain risks with using lawyers as investigators. An attorney who is directly involved in interviewing witnesses or gathering evidence may be a fact witness in a later suit, and thus may be disqualified from acting as the employer's attorney.

There are differences among lawyers, of course. Civil litigators can be useful but they don't necessarily make the best investigators as they sometimes tend to be predisposed to seek a certain result. A former prosecutor's investigative instincts may be preferable so long as they don't act too much like prosecutors.

If the attorney is involved in interviewing witnesses or directly gathering evidence, there may be a need to disclose the attorney's notes or have the attorney testify about his or her role in the investigation. In this situation, the attorney's advice to the company may not be legally privileged from disclosure, and opposing counsel may be able to force disclosure of all communications between the attorney and client regarding the subject of the investigation.

There may be a preference to have investigations conducted by your company's in-house counsel. The counsel's familiarity with the company, its policies, personnel and compliance politics is an advantage to the corporation. Investigations conducted by in-house counsel may be less costly and more efficient than one conducted by outside counsel. Employees may also be more willing to talk openly with in-house counsel than an outsider.

However, there exists the risk of perceived bias because your in-house counsel may be seen as a management representative, especially if a member of executive management or human resources is the subject. As company employees, they may appear less credible and independent. Credibility is essential to gain the confidence of investors and regulators when there is a suspicion of wrongdoing. There is an increased risk that in-house counsel may possess information that could make him a fact witness.

Outside counsel will sometimes be retained for the investigation to provide a quick response and to fill the need for additional resources. These lawyers can also help where the existing compliance staff and the company's internal lawyers do not have the subject-matter skills needed for the investigation. Whenever it is important to demonstrate that the fact finding was done by objective parties, it may be wiser to choose outside counsel.

Even if outside counsel is retained for your investigation, the investigation process should still be tailored to the same purposes as the in-house investigation. A sample guidance memorandum for outside counsel may be found in Appendix H.

Auditors and Accountants

If the investigation requires reviewing financial records and an understanding of business processes, using auditors and accountants seems obvious. Auditors can be used to review documentary evidence, evaluate tips or complaints, schedule losses, and provide assistance in technical areas of the company's operations. Auditors are the ones who frequently detect the financial anomalies. They can also identify fraud indicators.

Accountants, however, generally have limited fraud-investigation experience. Auditors and their accounting counterparts also may not be able to complete an investigation that requires more than straightforward "number crunching" or fraud that lies beneath what appears to be proper financial processes and documentation. If the scope of the investigation includes a larger perspective on the operative facts—especially if witnesses must be interviewed—these professionals are better used in collaboration with other investigators.

Corporate Security

Depending on the company, security department investigators are often assigned the field-work part of the investigation, including interviewing outside witnesses and obtaining public records and other documents from third parties. The drawbacks are that they often have little experience in workplace investigations and may have a limited view of the issues. Considering their day-to-day role, they may also attract unnecessary attention to the investigation.

Many companies hire former law-enforcement officers to work in their corporate security departments. This may appear sensible on one level. However, do not confuse the experience of someone enforcing public laws with that of investigating employee wrongdoing or asset protection. There is actually little crossover between the two areas, and the skills of one area may not effectively translate to the other.

Human Resources Personnel

The human resources department should be consulted to ensure that the laws governing the rights of employees in the workplace are not violated. Human resources personnel can also be useful if the claims involve allegations of discrimination or retaliation. Their involvement will lessen the possibility of a wrongful discharge suit or other civil claim.

However, remember that these personnel generally have limited expertise in the relevant legal areas. Also, their investigative skills and abilities may be limited because of the nature of their regular duties. Just because they have experience in human resources does not make them experienced fact-finders.

> **Process Pointer:** Resist the temptation to use any investigator. For best results, match their skills to the type of investigation you are conducting. Experience in human resources or law enforcement does not necessarily make someone an experienced workplace investigator.

Outsourcing the Investigation

For a workplace investigations unit, outsourcing can mean either the complete referral of an investigation to a third party, such as a law firm, or contracting out for selected or specialized investigative support services as needed. The decision to outsource is usually based on a cost-benefit analysis and the objectives of the investigation.

Outsourcing for specialized and expert services is almost always an important part of the budget and the approach to the workplace investigations process. The following are specialized services that are commonly used to support corporate investigations:

- Computer forensics
- Forensic auditing and accounting
- Handwriting analysis
- Document examination
- Surveillance
- Laboratory services
- Audio or video enhancement

I. Judging the Success of the Investigation

In the corporate context, how can you judge the effectiveness of your investigation? Is it a success if you found sufficient proof of misconduct? Or if you cleared someone? Or if you identified some process flaw in your company's operations? The answer to each of these questions is no.

The success of an investigation can be judged by its quality and relevance to the company's business needs, not just its findings. The quality of the investigation is judged by the quality of the final report and post-investigation actions. The relevance of the investigation depends on how it focused on the company's business goals and objectives, rather than on topics of corporate liability or similar risk. As stated elsewhere in this book, executive management takes risks all the time. Merely pointing out additional ones is not being all that helpful.

PART III

Conducting The Workplace Investigation

Now to the "nuts and bolts" of a workplace investigation. An important piece of advice is that "own" your investigations. You determine the manner in which the investigations will be conducted. Considering the goals, views and concerns of management is important, but you determine the investigation's contours.

Before getting started, you must remember your burden of proof. Proving misconduct through a workplace investigation is not a criminal trial. You are not held to the criminal-law standard of "beyond a reasonable doubt." Your company is a private employer, and your workers are likely at-will employees. The applicable standard here is the "preponderance of the evidence." This means: based on the information you have learned from the investigation, is it more likely than not that the implicated person committed the misconduct of which he is accused? Your company, of course, may adjust that standard higher based on its own particular needs or choices. But do not hamstrung yourself by making the mistake of comparing your standards to those of the local prosecutor.

> **Process Pointer:** Just like any other business process, this one has to be implemented fairly. Fairness for everyone is critical, especially for the implicated person because he has the most at risk.

"Owning" an investigation is the gold standard between a professional and a hack investigator. If you act as if you own the investigation, you are poised to offer true value to your company.

A. The Four Critical Steps

A properly conducted workplace investigation follows four steps:

Determine the nature of the allegation. You must gain a quick understanding of the problem. Usually, someone in the company knows the subject matter at issue and might even have personal knowledge of the incident. That person must be quickly debriefed so that you have some basis from which to proceed and a solid idea of how the matter under investigation evolved.

Develop the Facts. There are two basic components to a workplace investigation: interviews of employees or third parties, and the review of relevant documents. Document review is an important part of any investigation. Documents provide a historical narrative of events. They often tell much of the story by themselves. Also, they can provide a written framework into which information developed through witness interviews will fit.

Document the Investigation. To serve as a basis for management decisions, the investigation findings must be documented and supported. The report must give a comprehensive explanation of the information gathered in the course of the investigation. Sometimes a brief memorandum will suffice. In a complex investigation, a detailed written report will be prepared for presentation to executive management. The complexity of the issues and the stakes involved often dictate the way the investigation is documented.

Publish the Findings. Once completed, the investigation findings must be disclosed to management, the reporter and the implicated person. Of course, the level of detail will vary as necessary as will the document you produce, if at all, to each of them.

B. Understanding the Allegation

The Report

The report will come to you from a number of internal and external sources. (For convenience, we will assume the report came in through the company's whistleblower hotline.) Regardless of its source, you need sufficient information to provide probable cause that misconduct may have occurred. If so, then sufficient reason exists to begin an investigation.

You should be empowered to examine the raw facts to determine if either the source of the information or the combination of the source of the information and the then-available facts offer probable cause.

Meeting the Reporter

Your initial inquiry should be whether there is sufficient information to warrant an investigation. The investigation function must meet the first obligation of the process: to conduct an investigation only if one is truly needed. Essentially, the findings of the initial inquiry should seek to find more than a suspicion but less than a certainty of the truthfulness of the allegation. This criterion also reduces the likelihood that others will come to view the investigations process as a witch hunt.

If the reporter is not anonymous, contact them for additional information to determine whether probable cause exists. Generally, someone interviews the reporter to gather the operative facts fully and in more detail than the initial report. When conducting the intake interview, the interviewer should:

- Determine who, what, where, when, why and how.
- Ask the reporter with whom do they think the investigator should talk.
- Ask whom the reporter has spoken to about the issue.
- Ask what steps the reporter has taken to resolve or correct the issue.
- Ask whether the issue has affected the reporter's job in any way.
- Identify and request any relevant documents.
- Get as much detailed information as possible. A detailed first discussion helps to prepare a good, efficient investigation plan and reduces the number of times you may need to contact the reporter for more information.
- Not express opinions about the alleged conduct, and avoid opinions or comments about the character or ability of the others involved.
- Advise the reporter not to discuss the matter with others within the company except those with a need to know.
- Reassure the reporter that the company takes these complaints seriously and will determine whether an investigation is needed. Emphasize that no final conclusion will be reached until the investigation has been completed.

- If the reporter asks whether he will receive a copy of a final report of the investigation, the reporter should be informed that, although a final report will be prepared, the reporter will not receive a copy. Similarly, no specific, detailed report will be made to the reporter on management's response to the allegation.
- Advise the reporter to immediately report any possible acts of retaliation.
- Explain that, depending on the information that is learned, the investigation may be resolved at an informal stage rather than through a formal investigation.
- If the reporter says that he only wants to share his concerns but does not want an investigation conducted, inform the reporter that, depending on the information, your company may have a legal obligation to investigate the report.

> **Process Pointer:** Don't accept the reporter's characterization of the allegation at face value. You must analyze the facts you are offered and make your own determination regarding the category in which it fits. The report from the person who made the allegation is just a report. Offer no opinions to the reporter. At that time, you probably don't know the motives, personalities or histories of the people involved.

When making the decision to investigate, keep certain practical factors in mind. First, consider the source of the report. Some reporters are simply more credible than others. No reporter's allegations should be rejected out of hand, although issues of bias or self-interest must also be considered.

Second, consider the form of the report. Was it anonymous, or did it come from an identified party? Anonymous reports, however, should not be discounted unfairly. An anonymous report may be malicious, or it may be valid and accurate. Most employees do not trust management to keep their names confidential. Most people also do not want to be identified as the person responsible for bringing the matter to the attention of management. The detail provided in the anonymous report, or the lack of it, may either validate or invalidate the report. Keep an open mind and don't jump to conclusions.

> **Process Pointer:** Your company must accept anonymous complaints because you want maximum feedback on how your employees are acting properly. You need to remain attentive if someone tells you, even anonymously, that one of your employees could be engaging in misconduct.

Third, consider the substance of the report. Is it an employee-specific allegation, such as a payroll issue, that does not have systemic implications to the business? Or does it appear to be a process failure that impacts a significant operations issue? Is there a possible legal or criminal violation? Is it a violation of shared values? The substance of the report is a key factor in determining how to allocate resources in the investigation.

Fourth, determine whether there is sufficient information to determine if the allegations should be investigated. Additional inquiries should be made if additional facts are needed, the person raising the issue cannot supply the relevant facts, or there is a need to review documents.

Fifth, consider the credibility of the accusation. Have you received complaints like this before? Has this reporter made accusations in the past that demonstrate a motive other than to redress the matter? Does the reporter support the allegations with specific facts that show personal knowledge or furnish documents supporting their claims?

Keep in mind that in many situations, the nature and scope of the problem are not fully known at the time the report is reviewed. What may appear to be an isolated case of theft can really be a pattern of fraud against the company. Or vice versa. You will rarely know the full nature and scope of your problem at this time.

> **Process Pointer:** A failure to understand the complaint fully (what it includes and what it does not) can result in: a failure to investigate; a failure to investigate the right thing; a failure to talk to the right people; a failure to reach the right conclusion; and an over-reaction or under-reaction to the complaint. Do whatever it takes to get the story.

Deciding to Investigate

If you decide that a formal investigation is needed, you must answer some important questions. What will be the scope of the investigation? Who will conduct it? How much will it cost? The answers to these questions are not trivial because your responses may likely be viewed with hindsight by executive management, the press, the courts, and possibly the government.

There are certain benefits to deciding in favor of an investigation. These benefits include:

- A workplace investigation helps the company determine the extent of potential criminal or civil liability.
- If a company effectively investigates its own misconduct, the company may persuade the government to forego conducting a separate investigation, reduce the scope of its investigation, or allow the corporation to guide the government's investigation. A credible investigation may prevent a wide-ranging government investigation into the company's affairs.
- A director's fiduciary duty to the company includes the obligation to self-police, to establish compliance and detection programs.
- When there is a duty to investigate, the failure to do so may subject management to civil liability.
- The best way for the company to avoid indictment is to have full knowledge of all of the relevant facts so that an appropriate pre-indictment defense may be presented to the government. A thorough investigation, combined with voluntary disclosure, may be the dispositive factor in convincing the government not to bring criminal charges.
- A company can use a workplace investigation to minimize the effect of negative publicity that has arisen from allegations of wrongdoing. An investigation enhances the company's credibility now and in the future. The investigation distances the company from any wrongful acts by its employees, and the very existence of an investigation shows the company's good faith.
- A company may decide to investigate to encourage investor confidence and protect its position in the market. When allegations of misconduct are raised, the investigation may be used to address issues or dispel a cloud of suspicion.

However, consider the consequences of investigating the report. The investigation will require the commitment of time, resources and corporate energy, perhaps more than was initially expected or budgeted. There will be lost productivity in the business. People helping you will be diverted from their jobs. The internal machinery of the company will be explored and exposed. Executive management will have to live with the results of the investigation. This might include findings of fault, require public disclosure of the conduct, or the taking of internal or external remedial action.

While there is no hard and fast rule, generally the law, good business judgment and common sense favor conducting an investigation. Knowledge of the facts will enable management to examine options and respond effectively, and enable the company to decide whether it is necessary to disclose the findings to the government or publicly.

Deciding Not to Investigate

Not every allegation of misconduct must be investigated. If the initial investigation into the report fails to confirm that an incident has actually occurred or that there is a commercially reasonable basis for the incident complained about, there may be no basis for an investigation at that time. An investigation is generally not needed if:

- The report is a misunderstanding of company policy.
- The allegation relates to a lack of communication between the reporter and another person.
- No other facts are necessary to resolve the issue.
- The issue can be resolved informally, such as a request for assistance rather than an allegation of misconduct.

You must still document the report and the basis not to proceed. The record should show that, although no investigation was made, the reasons for not proceeding were commercially reasonable. If the investigation function is audited at some later time, the permanent record documents the handling of the matter and the inquiries you made at that time. The ability to account for all inquiries made is part of the ability to build a perception in management that there is a high degree of integrity in your function. The record also allows you to reopen the investigation if additional facts are obtained in the future that warrant further inquiries.

> **Process Pointer:** All the allegations must be documented or your workplace investigations unit will look like it just picks and chooses its investigations. If you choose not to investigate a report, you must document that fact and the reasons why you are not investigating.

Informing Management

When an investigation begins, you should inform your management. Because it is a business function, do not use clandestine or "James Bond" tactics, unless the circumstances of the investigation are so sensitive that there is no practical alternative. The investigative function will not be accepted by the managers you must cultivate as corporate allies if you are perceived as some secret police force snooping around unannounced. Similarly, you should be mindful of the effect on the future viability of your function if employees believe they are working in some corporate "police state." A template notification memorandum may be found in Appendix I.

Selecting which managers to inform is not based solely on finding someone who is not involved in the matter under investigation. A senior manager of the business unit involved should be informed about the nature of the investigation and its likely scope because, after all, he will be held accountable for your findings. The manager informed must also be of sufficient seniority to support the investigation's goals and neutralize any attempts by other managers to interfere with or impede the goals of the investigation. A sufficiently senior manager can also use their position to facilitate the availability of witness and the production of relevant documents. The manager informed should also be someone who will determine the action to be taken once the investigation's findings are disclosed. You should also consider who else in the company has a vested interest in the investigation and its outcome, such as legal counsel, Human Resources or the company's security department.

When informing management, a detailed description of the investigation plan is not necessary. However, alert them when significant events happen or if the scope of the investigation changes. Tell them about key investigative issues, especially those that may be provocative or embarrassing. This will allow managers time to prepare some internal response to those issues when challenged, and it will start them thinking about the possible impact of the investigation findings on their business's operations and structure.

You and management should have a clear understanding of what they hope the investigation should accomplish. Managing expectations is a crucial part of cultivating a relationship of confidence and value.

> **Process Pointer:** Manage the expectations of the business leader's carefully. Their perceptions of the investigation, the process and you depend on it. Counsel them regarding likely outcomes so they can prepare themselves accordingly.

Get Control of the Documents

The news that an investigation has begun will likely spread throughout the affected business unit. It might even become public knowledge. If the misconduct under investigation actually occurred, some employees may be tempted to destroy documents or computer files that show their involvement. The investigation will be compromised if this happens.

At the initial stages of the investigation, try to identify, with the help of the reporter if possible, the documents that are relevant to the investigation and the likely sources for those documents. Obtain these documents immediately.

Computer files should be immediately safeguarded. Consult your company's information-technology department to determine whether and to what extent server backups are done. Consider curtailing or shutting off access to company systems by employees under investigation.

Developing the Investigation Plan

You must be prepared to conduct a comprehensive, objective, fair and professional investigation. The planning needs to be flexible. The investigation may have to be expanded as information is developed.

The detail required, and the time consumed, to plan an investigation depends on its complexity. Routine investigations usually require a minimum amount of time and detail, and a simple outline or summary in a basic case-management system may be sufficient. More complex investigations need more time and require finely developed planning.

> **Process Pointer:** A broad investigation objective is more likely the sign of a poor investigation plan than a good one. People who cannot narrow the objective are likely unclear regarding their precise needs, so they cast the net wider hoping to catch their objective. All you need to investigate is whether the specific allegation against a specific person can be supported by the information you learn in the investigation.

A critical step in any investigation plan is to identify the precise reasons for the investigation. This must be defined early. Is the allegation related to a company policy only? If so, then the investigation would focus on the relevant facts, comparing that to the specified company policy, and then suggesting remedial action. If the investigation concerns criminal conduct or financial irregularities, then the investigation may also assess possible criminal and civil exposure for the company and the individuals involved.

To determine the scope of the investigation, consider each of the following factors:

- What specific misconduct or actions have been reported or alleged?
- Who is the source of the allegation?
- Does the allegation seem to be a plausible and legitimate concern?
- What are the initial facts?
- Are there any inconsistencies in the initial facts?
- What evidence suggests that the misconduct did not occur?
- Are there any mitigating circumstances?
- How serious does the potential violation appear to be?
- Is the scope broad enough to enable the company to take appropriate remedial action, including determining the extent to which internal processes should be modified?
- Will the investigation findings likely be reported to third parties such as law enforcement or regulators?

> **Process Pointer:** Resist the temptation to over-investigate. The burden of proof is not a criminal standard of "beyond a reasonable doubt." Otherwise, you will spend more time and resources than needed. You may also clear implicated people who should be removed from your company.

The scope of the investigation must also reinforce the fairness of the process. If the company must later defend a decision based on the investigation—a wrongful termination claim, for example—it will appear unreasonable for an employer to have reached a conclusion based on no evidence or no real investigation at all. Also, it will appear unfair if the company disciplines an employee based on weak evidence when better or stronger evidence is reasonably available but ignored.

Proper definition of the scope also protects the innocent. A properly conducted investigation will identify any wrongdoers, but that does not mean that other individuals might not be injured as a result of the fact-finding. The importance of defining the scope of an investigation is, in some ways, an effort to protect the innocent, to narrowly define the area to be investigation and to assure that those not involved in a particular act of misconduct are neither implicated by their proximity to the event nor exonerated by omission. A proper investigation determines the relevant facts, provides a basis for fixing accountability, and provides a basis for neutralizing rumors and innuendo.

Once the scope has been determined, make your plan. This is more than just a blueprint. It incorporates your proposed strategy. A proper strategy, regardless of the investigation's complexity, makes the investigation thorough and professional. The strategy of the investigation should move from the general to the specific, gradually zeroing in on the subject by carefully acquiring and analyzing information. As information is gathered, your theory can be refined to focus the investigation on the most logical source of misconduct and/or business process failure.

An investigation plan ensures that the company has met its obligations to the subject of the investigation, to the proper operations of the business, and to the company's shareholders. Although there is no precise format, a good investigation plan considers each of the following issues and questions:

- The business unit or function involved.
- The alleged facts and behavior that led to the investigation. This can be set out in a chronology of events which can then be enlarged as the investigation develops.
- The company employees who are the subject of the investigation.
- What law, policies, procedures, codes of conduct or other requirements may have been violated, and where documents specifying those requirements can be located?
- How widespread is the misconduct? Is this an isolated occurrence or a systemic problem?
- What information will be sought on each issue, and who are the potential sources of that information?
- What type of report should be prepared to publish the findings?
- After the investigation is completed, what post-investigation steps are likely to be needed?
- Which individuals might have personal knowledge of the about one or more of the factual issues.
- The order in which witnesses should be interviewed.
- What specific issues are to be covered with each witness?
- What documents will be needed to conduct the investigation and complete the investigation file?
- What documents will be shown to each witness, and which documents will be sought from each witness?
- Which senior managers will receive the reported findings, and to whom will the investigative team report?

There are serious consequences if the investigation is too narrow or too broad. You need to get to the root cause of the problem and not just deal with its symptoms. If the investigation is superficial, the business problem will not be addressed, and the workplace will be exposed to further disruption. However, an overly broad investigation can equally harm the workplace culture and disrupt the business.

As the investigation proceeds, be flexible to changes in the plan. Situations change, and you have to able to adapt. The true nature of the problem under investigation may turn out to be different from what you first thought. Do not let the investigation process become so rigid that you can't alter it when necessary.

If you change the investigation objectives, add a contemporaneous note to the file documenting the new objectives and your reasons for changing them. This could help you later on if you are accused of some improper motive for changing. You must protect the process from being put on trial by the implicated person.

> **Process Pointer:** An investigation plan does not have to be formal, but set the scope properly so you will have the right parameters to guide you. You always must be prepared to explain why you did what you did. Never put yourself in the position of explaining your plan by saying that you never considered any other course of action.

C. The Investigator's Protocol

The workplace investigative process is less threatening to business colleagues if you also formulate a standard operating protocol and the business colleagues become reassured that there are no surprises to fear. A sample protocol may be found in Appendix J. Understanding key investigations concepts ensures that the workplace investigations process will survive the political forces which exist in any corporation.

The Right to Investigate Misconduct

Each employer must ensure that the rules of conduct are followed by its employees. These rules prohibit some acts and require others. Known or suspected violations become the subject matter of an investigation.

The right of an employer to conduct an investigation exists because executive management is accountable to the shareholders for the use of company assets. The employer has a privilege, and in some cases a duty, to investigate employee wrongdoing. The company's right to investigate arises from the duty to protect the company's business, other employees and the public from wrongdoing employees.

Obligations of the Investigator

You are a company employee. The company has a profit motive. Therefore, your duties must be performed with the minimum possible disruption to the business operation. A good investigator balances his duties with the need to keep the business flow going.

You must also assure that the investigation reasonably protects the rights of all individuals involved. This includes the recognition that while the employer has a duty to investigate, there also exists a right of privacy for the implicated employee. You must know that, in many cases, the fact-gathering process must establish the facts of the matter without the participation of the implicated employee.

You must protect the reputations and similar interests of those who participate in the investigation. Even the fact-finding of a properly conducted investigation might injure someone, however unintentionally. The importance of defining the scope of an investigation is, for example, partly an effort to protect the innocent.

Your personal conduct in gathering information and evidence affects the credibility of the process. When the investigation is complete, business managers must determine whether to accept the information elicited as the facts of the matter and the truth of what happened. You must assure that these managers have the opportunity to recognize the relative strengths of the various pieces of information and to make a decision.

You are the one most responsible in an investigation for offering management the broadest array of alternative actions to bring the matter under investigation to a logical conclusion. Your individual performance must not jeopardize the availability of these options. You get only one opportunity to draw conclusions based on the information you gathered.

Respecting Employee Rights

You must be prepared to respond to concerns from employees who are reluctant to be interviewed. An employee asked to participate in an investigative interview generally has little choice. Employees are required to cooperate with your investigation as a result of an employee's general duty of loyalty to their employer. Refusal to do so may result in discipline or even termination.

An employee's resistance may also come in the form of a literal or figurative assertion of the Fifth Amendment privilege against self-incrimination. However, this privilege does not apply in the context of private employment. Similarly, private employers generally are not liable under federal or state law for violating the employee's constitutional rights because there is no governmental action.

> **Process Pointer:** The investigations process is more important than the success of any particular case. No matter how critical an effective investigation of a particular allegation may seem, do not compromise your standards. The cost to the workplace investigations unit will be higher than the value you try to achieve through unusual tactics. It takes only a moment to destroy the ethical credibility of your unit.

Investigator Best Practices

Investigating is equal parts of art and science. The best techniques needed to investigate allegations of workplace misconduct vary, and the techniques reflect the strengths and personality of the investigator using them. However, better investigations follow similar practices:

Be fair and objective. Everyone involved in an investigation deserves to be treated with respect and dignity. This protects the legitimacy of the investigations process. Under typical circumstances, the implicated person will receive reasonable notice of the report and be offered a real opportunity to respond.

Remember that, in the context of an investigation, words have special meanings. An investigation is not an inquisition. The person who brings a matter to your attention is a "reporter." The report is not a complaint or claim. If the report is made regarding someone, that person is a "subject" of the investigation (or the "implicated person"), not a target. Using proper terminology reinforces the investigator's role as a business-oriented truth gatherer and not a prosecutor.

A common investigator error is to pre-judge the outcome of an investigation before all the witnesses have been interviewed and all the relevant documents have been reviewed. Healthy doubt is a good trait. Good investigators resist the temptation to jump to any conclusions. It could cloud your judgment. Until the report has been proven or a suspicion validated, there is no confirmation of wrongdoing. Nor should a report be dismissed simply based on your opinion of the source. Keep an open mind to other possible explanations or scenarios.

Be sensitive to any actual or perceived conflicts of interest that might arise when you make your inquiries. Avoid even the appearance of bias or partiality to a particular person or result. If you believe that an actual or perceived conflict exists—such as if you know the people involved in some way that might compromise your objectivity or you have some interest in the matter being investigated stop and inform the Investigations Manager immediately.

Seek maximum cooperation from your witnesses. Full, voluntary cooperation may be hard to get, but the goal should be to get witnesses to go beyond the basis and give as complete a picture as possible. This includes suggesting other people with whom to speak.

Keep the interviews serious and business-like. Investigations are a serious process. Remain calm and in control throughout the interview. There is no place for joking, sarcasm or threats. People involved in an investigation are generally apprehensive about the issues involved and the possible consequences. Recognize the significance of your work and its potential impact. People, including those in executive positions, could lose their jobs as a result of your inquiry.

A good interviewer never stoops to undignified tactics. At times, the investigator may need to be aggressive or tenacious, but never insulting or demeaning. There are times in an interview when an investigator will not be treated politely. Despite the hurt and angry feelings such conduct may evoke in us, you cannot yourself to that level. If you become angry, insulted or offended during an interview, he gives up control of the interview.

Never mislead a witness. This will result in employees distrusting the entire compliance process—exactly the opposite atmosphere you are trying to create.

Do not discuss your opinions or conclusions. The witness does not need to know what you think.

Protect the confidentiality of the investigation. Allegations of misconduct, even if later found to be groundless, can still damage someone's reputation. Do not disclose the allegations or the existence of an investigation to anyone without a need to know. Curiosity by others, including executive management, is not a basis for sharing information about an investigation. The inadvertent disclosure of information could lead to the subject employee bringing claims for defamation or infliction of emotional distress. Sensitive or confidential information should not be disclosed to witnesses during the course of the investigation.

Make the inquiries promptly, but take the time needed to exercise appropriate diligence. Make sure the inquiries are made timely to ensure that appropriate documents and e-mails are preserved, and that all steps are taken to stop continuing or imminent noncompliance.

Take all steps necessary to protect whistleblowers and those who cooperate in the investigation. Avoid disclosing to the witness the source of the report. Any report of retaliation that emerges during the investigation should be treated as an additional report of noncompliance and reported to the Investigations Manager immediately.

When making inquiries, consider the broader implications of what you have discovered for the affected business unit or the company as a whole. In addition to making recommendations to management about what, if any, action should be taken with regard to the person involved, recommend appropriate changes to policies, procedures, training, monitoring, audits, or other steps to prevent a recurrence. Before making recommendations regarding systemic changes, consider what the underlying causes of the problems were. The investigation should be used to improve the business.

> **Process Pointer:** No one expects perfection, but everyone expects fairness. Never do anything that you would not be prepared to explain to the CEO of your company and say "you're damn right I did."
>
> Prejudging the outcome also causes problems because it closes your mind to other possibilities, explanations, and participants. You could easily miss a bigger investigative picture because you were too focused on the limited scope of your current inquiry.

D. The Personal Interview

While documents may give you the clearest record of key events, the most revealing information comes from employees. The key elements of almost every workplace investigation are the employee interviews.

Employees are sources of tremendous information to investigators. When they cooperate, they can explain relevant facts and interpret relevant documents. They can give insights into management styles and corporate cultures that put specific employee conduct into context. Sample requests for employee interviews may be found in Appendices K and L.

All information can be grouped into two areas: trivial and important. The important information is the information offered in response to "who, what, where, when, why and how" questions. It also includes both unusual observations and the interviewer's gut reactions.

Interviews always involve a relationship between two people: the interviewer and the witness. The witness, one way or another, has to be convinced that talking to the investigator is the most important thing they should be doing at the time.

Interviews need to maintain focus. It is essential to keep the witness focused on the matters under discussion and not allow rambling thoughts and comments. Proper planning of the interview can avoid this.

The witness may be reluctant to provide the needed information, or to cooperate. In these situations, you have a two-step task: first, to make the subject willing to cooperate with the questioning, and secondly, to interview him. This is your challenge. There are a number of ways you may get the witness' cooperation:

- Ask general questions.
- Explain the advantages of cooperation.
- Downplay the disadvantages of non-cooperation.
- Play on their conscience.
- Speak their language and empathize.
- Give them a chance to explain.

Whatever the methods, the basic idea is to develop your own rapport with the witness. This creates a connection between you, and it then becomes possible to create a change in the behavior of the witness. The dynamics of rapport constitute the foundation of the inquiry-persuasion process. It allows you to enter the world of the witness.

> **Process Pointer:** Interview only those people for which you need to fill factual gaps. Decide early on what exactly need to know and who can best give it to you. Do not look for witnesses whose information does nothing more than repeat credible information that you already know. These other witnesses may have differing recollections and send you off on irrelevant tangents.
>
> Before interviewing anyone, decide who likely has the information you need and who is likely to give it to you. Don't assume that everyone will cooperate and tell you the truth. People can lie or be reluctant to cooperate for a variety of motives, including nothing more than a desire not to get involved.

Who to Interview

A natural temptation is to think that the more people you speak to, the more complete the investigation will be. Resist the temptation. Interviewing everyone is a sure sign that you do not have an investigation strategy.

The existence of the investigation is disruptive, so you want to minimize the amount you distract the business unit from doing their daily jobs. Also, the more people you speak to, the more likely it is that the information you discuss in the interviews will get shared and circulated, thereby tainting the quality of the information you get later on from other people. Finally, because perceptions and motivations differ from person to person, you risk muddling up your findings with conflicting statements and recollections that you now have to reconcile.

The workplace investigation is intended to determine whether an allegation of misconduct can be substantiated by the facts learned through the investigation process. Because it is a very limited inquiry, you only need to talk to people who fall within three categories:

Information provider: an individual, often without first-hand knowledge, often with some technical competence, who can explain certain matters which are relevant to the investigation. The accounts payable person who explains how vendor invoices are processed and company checks printed, or the IT person who explains how e-mails are stored on the company's computer servers are good examples.

Witness: an individual who has observed some activity that is relevant to the investigation and can, from his own recollection and personal knowledge, give you information regarding their observations. An office co-worker who saw the misconduct happen is a good example.

Subject: an individual who, based on the available information, is considered to be the principal implicated person in the investigation.

In a workplace investigation, generally plan to interview the following people:

- The reporter (if identified).
- The subject of the investigation.
- Anyone who observed a relevant incident.
- Other witnesses with relevant information, whether identified by the complaining employee or the subject.

- Authors of relevant documents.
- The supervisor of the subject.
- People whom the reporter has asked you to interview.
- People whom the subject has asked you to interview. (This is not only to get potentially relevant information. Interviewing these people reinforces the procedural fairness of the process by facilitating the subject's efforts to respond to the allegations.)

Stay focused on the limited scope of the investigation. Seek interviews with those people who have first-hand knowledge of the situation.

> **Process Pointer:** Pick a witness who can be the "storyteller." This person gives you the fullest picture of the investigation facts. You can then use this information as the framework for other witnesses. The others will fill in the facts and bolster the ones you know.

Order of Interviews

As a general rule, documents should be examined before interviews begin. This will give you an understanding of the potential evidentiary value of the investigation, as well as to protect the security of documents. It will also allow you to understand the nature of the matters at issue, to identify key players, and to plan for interviews.

Because the investigation has begun, we will assume that you have already interviewed the reporter to determine if probable cause existed to begin the investigation. It is then often best to work with people having the most facts first, then branching out to interview those who can complete the investigation picture by providing supplemental information.

In general, the implicated person is interviewed last. There will be a temptation to confront and/or suspend those suspected of misconduct. However, this must be balanced against the extent to which critical fact-finding will be impeded at an early stage of the investigation. Pre-confrontation investigation will uncover important facts reflecting the nature and extent of the misconduct, allowing the company to assess the actual harm. Facts which directly or circumstantially implicate the investigation subject may also be uncovered. This will enhance the likelihood that the later confrontation will be successful. Also, before the confrontation, the company must consider the legality of certain investigation techniques, the subject's rights and the business implications if the employee is dismissed. Only by carefully considering these issues in advance can you effectively design a strategy for confronting the employee.

Even if it is believed that the implicated person will not offer a confession and will likely deny the allegations, an interview is still necessary. Inform the implicated person's immediate supervisor of the report and your intention to interview the individual. Ask their supervisor to be vigilant for further problems, retaliation or other reactions which may affect the investigation. The implicated person should be given full—or as full as reasonably possible—information about the report against him and a full opportunity to explain and defend against the allegations. Reinforce the fairness of the process by giving the implicated person every opportunity to explain his or her actions.

In some circumstances, however, it may be best to conduct interviews without advance warning. Surprise interviews may be necessary when there is a concern that witnesses will alter or destroy evidence or that witnesses will confer with each other in an attempt to make their accounts consistent.

If all else fails, begin at the bottom and work up the chain of responsibility rather than begin at the top and work down. Productive sources can always be re-interviewed later to ask follow-up questions.

> **Process Pointer:** Honest people have little tolerance for theft. A dishonest person may be more sympathetic when hearing about an incident, speculating that the wrongdoer possibly had a good reason for doing it.
>
> Keep in mind that employees rarely volunteer information about wrongdoing. Even innocent employees who observed but did not participate in the misconduct will be uncomfortable discussing it. It may be the taboo against "ratting" on others, or it may be a concern that you may consider them a participant as well. But when the right questions are asked, the information will come out. Misconduct is hard to conceal.

Collecting Information from Third Parties

Some investigations will include interviews with third parties such as vendors or former employees. Approach these witnesses cautiously. Consider whether a company representative who knows the witness should make the initial contact on your behalf. Be careful to avoid disclosing confidential or fault-related issues to the witness. Remain vigilant to avoid compromising the protections of any applicable legal privileges.

Ideally, third-party witnesses should not be interviewed until after you have obtained as much information as possible from internal sources. This will allow you to disclose only those issues for which the witness becomes a critical source of information. It also reduces the risk that you will become at the mercy of the third party for their cooperation with the investigation.

Where to Conduct the Interview

The place in which the interview occurs affects the interview's effectiveness. An interviewee who fears that his co-workers may hear what he says or see him speaking to you is not going to give you all the information you might otherwise gather. Conversely, an interviewee who feels very comfortable and protected in his statements is likely to share more with you than even they may have intended. After all, once people start speaking comfortably, their natural protective defenses begin to drop and the information starts flowing.

The location of the interview should be a neutral place that is conducive to effective information-gathering and protects the fairness of the process. Pursue an interview and not a criminal interrogation. It should be a relatively benign environment, and the witness should be physically free to get up and leave at any time. The room should be at normal temperature and should be free of distractions. Forget the stereotype of the bare room, single chair and spotlight.

Interviews in restaurants or other public places should be only used as a last resort because there are too many distractions and risks to confidentiality. However, they can put a witness at ease because of its public, non-worksite nature. Off-site and home visits can be useful, however, when you need to gain the witness' cooperation to further the objectives of the investigation. Maintaining the secrecy of the interview enables the investigation to remain secret if the witness agrees to cooperate. An off-site location might also be chosen if there is any concern about violence or other disruption in the workplace as a result of confronting the witness.

Telephone interviews should be done as a last resort because the witness controls his or her setting, and the investigator cannot observe the witness' body language. You may not even be aware that someone else may be monitoring the conversation or feeding responses to the witness.

> **Process Pointer:** Remember that in-office interviews announce to everyone that you are there and that the company takes the matter seriously.

Interview Dynamics

Every human interaction has interpersonal dynamics. So do interviews. In an interview, you must gain and continually control the discussion. If you do not control the witness, the witness will likely divert the interview process, leading the interview in directions the witness chooses. Worse, the witness can become the interviewer.

In an interview, control simply means the ability to get the witness to respond. Response is the key element. The witness will always respond somehow. The critical issue is whether the witness will respond as you want. Control over the interview is derived from your ability to persuade the witness to respond in the desired manner. An interview should be neither an argument nor a debate.

Never get angry if the witness becomes difficult and frustrating. Becoming angry amounts to giving control of your emotions to the witness, which is the opposite of your goal—to control the witness' emotions. If you cannot control your own emotions, you cannot control the witness. Whatever the implicated person did, he did not do it to you personally. (And if they did, you should not be conducting the investigation.) Recognize the investigation as a business problem that needs to be resolved in a business-like manner.

Preparing for the Interview

Preparing for the interview is essential. The investigator has to do their homework. The preparation will not only help the investigation. It will convey to the witness that the investigator is thoroughly interested in the matter under investigation.

As a practical matter, speak to a witness only once. An interview should be a planned procedure, so each interview involves the development of a plan. The witness—and especially the subject of the investigation—likely anticipates what you will discuss. It is easy to overlook an important issue if interviews are conducted without careful focus on the issues to be addressed.

> **Process Pointer:** Some interviewers make the mistake of not preparing in advance, especially those with plenty of experience. This is wrong. If you are not already sure what you are going to ask the witness, you are more than likely not to get the information you need. Just jot down the key areas you want to explore.

Carefully consider what questions will be asked and what statements will be made at the start and close of the interview, and how you will document both the information obtained from and the instruction and assurances provided to the witness. Draft in advance an outline of the remarks that will be made in an opening statement, a preliminary list of questions to be asked (but not a script), and a checklist of instructions appropriate to the person being interviewed.

Prepare your outline before each interview. Sometimes you will be able to use the same outline with several witnesses. Nonetheless, you should review it before interviewing each witness. The exercise of preparing the outline forces you to think through what information this witness is most likely to have and how that information fits into the rest of your investigation. The outline also lets you think about the most effective order of questioning. Don't forget that planning an interview also means that you also consider when you should ask a question. You usually can get favorable information from a witness more effectively if you ask those questions before you ask the ones that are more confrontational.

Be thoroughly familiar with the substance of the investigation. Once the interview begins, the investigator who lacks a working knowledge of the issues involved will have difficulty identifying discrepancies or omissions in the witness' statements. Also, there is a tendency for an uninformed investigator to look at paper instead of people. Once the interview begins, all new information is going to come from the witness, not the file.

To the extent possible, know everything possible about the witness. They could be a good source of institutional knowledge about the company or the business processes involved. You might want to identify whether they might have some motive that affects their credibility. It may also help you detect if they are evading meaningful responses to issues about which they should know. Moreover, it helps you ensure that, because the interview will be as complete as you can make it, the scope of the investigation remains properly calibrated to the allegation under investigation.

> **Process Pointer:** If you prepare well, then the witness' information will help you understand the case better and refine your hypothesis. Otherwise, the interview becomes little more than asking questions and writing down the answers. Do the hard work early on, and you won't have to do it later.

The Interview Itself

Most of the employees you interview will be nervous and understandably apprehensive. You should briefly explain at the start of the interview what is going on and what is expected of the witness.

The introduction to the interview is the hardest part because you have to create the proper impression, enlist the witness' cooperation and explain the nature of your inquiry, all at once.

Read the "Instructions for Witnesses" aloud to the witness. These should be your standard ground rules for the interview. The instructions establish the conventions and assumptions between the parties. These instructions are may be found in Appendix M. Be prepared, as a preliminary matter, to answer any questions the witness may have about the interview.

Giving clear interview instructions not only lays the ground rules. It also conveys to the witness that you are in control of the interview and they are not.

The witness should receive a brief explanation of the matter under investigation. Explain why the witness has been included in the investigation (e.g., that they have been identified as someone with a report, have been subject of misconduct, or have been identified as someone who may have information relevant to the investigation).

There are certain initial standard questions that you should ask the witness. It is important to know:

- The witness' full name.
- Job title, duties, and times worked.
- Start and end dates of employment.
- Supervisor's name and title.
- The identity of any employees who report directly to the witness.
- Whether the witness has been previously investigated or disciplined.
- What the witness has already been told by others interviewed or involved in the matter.
- What the witness has been told by supervisors or management.
- Whether the witness has been threatened in any way to provide or withhold testimony.

Do not stress time limits on the interview. The witness should never be given the impression that there is a time limit. Make the witness believe that the company is sufficiently concerned about the matter. Conversely, do not accept unreasonable limits that would interfere with their ability to conduct a professional interview.

Employees often ask whether they are in trouble or whether they will be disciplined. Be straightforward—it is certainly possible that employees may be disciplined if they engage in misconduct, but at this point in the investigation you are just gathering the facts. Never represent to a witness that their cooperation may be offered as a quid pro quo for avoiding any disciplinary, civil or criminal action.

A witness may ask if he needs a lawyer. Offer no opinion on that. Management is not required to allow interview subjects to have a lawyer and can insist that the interview continue with the witness without a lawyer present. However, if the witness insists on having a lawyer present, stop the interview at this point.

Most interviewers find it helpful to take a break when conducting interviews. The longer or more complex an interview is, the more valuable a break can be. Breaks should probably be taken at least every 90 minutes.

It should be taken at a natural spot, not in the middle of the witness's explanations, but usually when you feel that you have obtained almost all the information you need on a particular point.

> **Process Pointer:** Tape recording sounds tempting, but it will have a chilling effect on both you and the witness. It is also unnecessary. Proper note taking and a timely accurate interview memorandum will sufficiently memorialize the conversation.
>
> Similarly, having an administrative person in the room to take notes is a bad idea. The note taker will likely miss something important or misquote something. Then the notes will be used as proof as to what was or wasn't said. The second problem is that it double-teams the interview, making the witness more uncomfortable.

Asking the Best Questions

Witness interviews are neither pretrial depositions nor courtroom cross-examinations. The purpose of the interview is to elicit truthful and relevant information. Phrase questions and ask them in a manner designed to achieve that purpose. Investigators should never talk down to a witness or use language that the person cannot understand. They should use language that the witness understands, and as the interview proceeds, they should ensure that the witness does understand the exact meaning of the words they are using.

> **Process Pointer:** Don't let the witness use legalistic works like "unethical," "assault," "battery," etc. The witness may not know the exact meaning—or the implications—of legal terms. You should not use them either, even if you know their precise meaning. The terms could be loaded with emotional baggage that would overwhelm the witness.

Remember the 80:20 rule. You are there to acquire knowledge, not disclose it. The witness should be talking 80 percent of the time, and the investigator only approximately 20 percent of the time. The two most common interviewing errors are (i) the interviewer does not allow the witness to tell his own story, and (ii) the interviewer talks too much.

The interview should center on the specific misconduct at which the investigation is aimed. Transforming the interview into a wide-ranging inquisition into all possible areas of misconduct is counterproductive because it detracts from the focus of the investigation.

The initial discovery of misconduct may be just a symptom of a much larger problem. Keep alert to that possibility and be prepared to expand your questions accordingly.

Sometimes, managers may want to participate in, or attend, interviews of various witnesses. This can have a chilling effect on the witness. Conduct the interviews of employees without their managers present.

Use a non-confrontational approach. A witness is more likely to cooperate with someone he likes, or at least feel reasonably comfortable with, rather than someone he considers threatening. There may be times when it is necessary to take a more harsh approach. Nonetheless, in the first instance, it is almost always beneficial to try a more disarming approach.

Ask questions in chronological or other systematic order, not randomly. If questioning is confusing, you will lose the witness's train of thought and risk missing information.

Do not expect the witness to have an exact recollection of events that occurred some time ago. It is your obligation to refresh the witness' recollection with documents or other information, if needed.

There are no "magic questions" to ask when interviewing someone. But you will never fail if you ask the "who, what, where, when, why and how" questions. However, avoid asking "why" questions until the end. These questions are usually antagonistic because they sound moralistic.

Ask open-ended questions. Open-ended questions are more likely to result in your learning what the witness knows. "Who was there?" "What was said?" "Why did you do that?" Open-ended questions encourage the witness to respond. They allow you to learn about the subject, based on how the witness describes himself. They also help the witness relax.

Do not ask close-ended questions. This type of question tends to require a "yes" or "no," or a brief statement at most. These questions do not provide for extended responses and, as a rule, will not let the witness relax. The witness is more likely to provide the answer and then stop talking.

Ask straightforward questions. Do not be cute, tricky or shrewd. Your goal is to get information in the simplest, clearest way possible.

The basis of the witness' knowledge is always important. Determine whether the witness is speaking from personal knowledge or just relying on the hearsay statements of others. "How do you know that?" is a question to ask often.

Ask the witness to list all individuals who have knowledge of any of the events. "Who else might know?" is a question to ask often.

Distinguish between words used by the witness and situations where the witness simply agrees with a question or statement. Consider the wording of leading questions and whose words were used. Identify situations where there were only agreements with statements you made or where the witness made the actual statements. Allow the witness to reject your characterization if they don't accept it. You want the most accurate recollections possible.

The investigation should identify any mitigating circumstances that may affect the assessment of fault, such as personal or health problems.

It may not always be possible, but try to structure questions in a way that does not call attention to particular problem areas. The order of questions as well as your demeanor in asking them can alert a witness to the focus and severity of the problem being investigation. If there is something you would prefer to remain highly confidential, take care in structuring and asking the questions to the witness. (Some experienced investigators even include subjects of no real relevance to avoid tipping the witness off to the nature of the inquiry.)

Save unfriendly or embarrassing questions until the end of the interview. Beginning with the "tough" questions may cause the witness to become defensive.

On key factual questions it can be valuable to return to the same question more than once in different ways. People often remember things in waves, and this approach may develop additional detail.

If a person does not remember, try to help by asking questions that help recreate the situation when the event occurred, but do not suggest an answer.

Empathy is important. This is the feeling associated with emotional identification with another person. When used correctly, this mutual concern encourages the free flow of information. Take a non-judgmental attitude, and be careful to disguise any negative feelings or lack of compassion for the witness.

Silence is a great technique. Many people cannot stand silence and find this unnerving. They will fill up the void with talk, often saying something they had no intention of revealing. The average person expects no more than seven seconds of silence during a conversation. If you don't say anything after the witness answers a question, the witness will frequently give the investigator more information than he intended to give you. The silence effectively pressured the subject into offering more information by communicating that the investigator felt that the answer was not complete. Silence can also be an effective way to undermine a witness who is cocky and confident in his or her own ability to control the discussion. The witness, and not you, should become uncomfortable with the silence.

Avoid doing anything that might be taken as an attempt to influence the witness' answers. Avoid characterizing the company's position, summarizing the statements of other witnesses, or selectively presenting documents in a way that may distort the facts. Misleading a witness, even unintentionally, undermines the value of their information.

There is always the possibility that the information the witness is providing contradicts either something they said earlier or a piece of information gathered from another source. One of the most effective techniques is to note the contradictions and than, at the appropriate point, ask the witness how these contradictory facts could be true (or reconciled). Recall them individually and review the facts again.

Ask again at the end of the interview: "Is there anything else relevant to this matter that I should know? Is there anything I missed? What else should I ask the investigator? What other documents are important? Who else knows about this? Who else can help me with this information? Is there a question I should have asked and didn't? Is there anything else you know about this?" Ask several of these questions. It is very important to document these questions to support the fact that the witness was asked for all relevant information.

> **Process Pointer:** Don't write your questions in advance. You will lock yourself into only the points your questions cover. If the witness discusses something interesting that is not in your script, you will likely ignore it. Also, a script will make you more concerned about your questions rather than the witness' answers.
>
> Take your time. If you finish the interview but think you did not get all the facts you could have, you likely rushed through it.

Facilitators of communication

Facilitators of communication are the forces that make conversations easier to accomplish. These dynamics play a role in every conversation, including a risk-assessment interview. There are six common facilitators:

- *Fulfilling expectations.* When people communicate, they communicate their expectations of what they want the other person to do. (Nodding your head in agreement is one such way.) The interviewer communicates his expectations to the employee, such as an expectation of cooperation and truth-telling.
- *Recognition.* Everyone needs the recognition and esteem of others. People "perform" in exchange for recognition and other social rewards. Interviewers who acknowledge the contributions of the employees will get better results.
- *Altruistic appeals.* People need to identify with a higher value besides self interest. Altruistic feelings increase a person's self-esteem through association.
- *Sympathetic understanding.* People need the sympathy of others and share their joys, fears, successes and failures. This is not recognition for esteem as much as a common humanity. Empathy leads to an emotional identification with another person. When used correctly, the mutual concern facilitates the free flow of information.
- *Catharsis.* This is a release from unpleasant emotional tensions. People feel better talking about something that bothers them.
- *Extrinsic rewards.* An employee may be motivated by more than a desire to be helpful to the investigation. The reward could be money, privileges or prestige.

Just as some dynamics facilitate communication, some factors inhibit it:

- *Ego threat.* This dynamic actually has three parts.
  Repression—An employee who did the wrong thing may be denying it to themselves too. They may have subconsciously forgotten it. (This happens with embezzlers because they may repress what they did because it conflicts with their moral code)
  Disapproval—An employee may have information but they may not want to tell you because they feel that you will condemn them.
  Loss of status—An employee may fear a loss of status if the information comes out.

- *Etiquette.* Some answers would be considered in poor taste or things that are not discussed in front of women. The interviewer can address this factor by anticipating the setting for the interview.
- *Trauma.* This is an acutely unpleasant feeling associated with reporting the experience.
- *Forgetting.* This is a frequent obstacle. It can be related to the original emotional impact of the event and the degree it relates to a person's ego. Another factor is the time that has elapsed. Another factor is the nature of the interview setting.

> **Process Pointer:** Don't overlook the possibility that a witness' resistance may be based on a fear of retaliation. If the witness does not want to "rat" on a friend, instruct the witness that you are just a fact gatherer trying to learn as much as you can. Remind them that someone else is the judge and jury.

Having the Gall to Ask

Investigations require you to ask uncomfortable questions to witnesses. Unfortunately, this is unavoidable, and investigators should embrace this reality.

In many investigations, the issues you are investigating are provocative. Someone may be fired. Someone may not want to implicate another person. Someone may have done something terrible. But you have to know about it.

It is a normal human reaction to want to avoid asking tough or embarrassing questions. It takes a certain amount of gall to ask someone if they stole money, if they sent erotic messages to a co-worker, if they forged company records. But conducting a proper investigation requires you to be brave enough to ask questions that would be rude and intrusive in other situations. To justify asking the questions, the participants should agree before you ask them that these questions are necessary for the investigation.

Do not be reluctant to make the person uncomfortable. It is your job to find out the truth and make it hard for anyone to tell you anything less.

The Written Statement

Statements play an important role in investigations. If the witness has been handled right, the witness may not likely object to offering a written statement.

Invite the witness to submit a written personal statement of the relevant facts. (This is included in the witness instructions, and a template form may be found in Appendix N.) This statement is not the same as a voluntary statement furnished by someone making a confession. This statement is intended to reinforce the procedural fairness of the investigation. The statement should contain a record of the issues raised, the witness' version of what happened, who was involved, witnesses, dates, etc. The statement should also respond to or explain any evidence. Your questions necessarily reflect those matters about which you want information. The witness statement, by contrast, reflects what the witness wants to say about the matter. The written statement may give you additional information about the investigation. The written statement should be signed, dated and added to the investigation file.

Closing the Interview

The interview should be closed on a positive note. Use this opportunity to review key facts elicited during the interview to be certain these points were correctly understood.

At the end of the interview, thank the witness for the information furnished. Give the witness your telephone number if more information becomes available or is remembered. Keep the door open for future contact if they would like to add or change anything. The goal is to obtain the most accurate information possible. An interview is not intended to be a memory test.

If you asked the witness to furnish documents, renew that request and agree to a list and date for production, if possible, of the needed documents. Consider giving the witness a written list of the items he has to furnish. Follow up a few days later to confirm the request.

Tell the witness that appropriate management personnel will make any final determination regarding the best way to resolve the issue, but stress that that the witness' input is valuable and will be considered seriously. The witness should be told that the results of the investigation remain confidential and that the specific corrective actions may not be communicated to the witness.

The interview does not need to have covered all the facts, events and conduct. All you need to move forward are the basic elements of the conduct alleged.

> **Process Pointer:** Retain goodwill. In closing the interview, take the time to preserve the rapport with the witness. You may need to contact them again. They can also become advocates of your investigation process.
>
> Stay alert to communications inhibitors such as time demands, threats to the witness' ego, trauma and memory lapses. Be prepared to navigate around them.
>
> Remember the things that facilitate communication: recognition, altruistic appeals, sympathy and catharsis. Use these to keep the information flowing.

E. Interviewing the Implicated Employee

The workplace investigations process is obligated to provide the implicated person with the opportunity to defend himself against the allegations. When you properly interview the implicated person, you fulfill any fundamental-fairness rights that he might enjoy, and if he admits to wrongdoing, that statement can be used as proof of guilt.

The Right to Respond

The implicated person should be reasonably provided with an opportunity to respond to the allegation and the information developed against him. If the implicated person denies the allegation, he should be offered the opportunity to assist in the investigation to establish his innocence. Even if the weight of the information uncovered tends to substantiate the allegation, the investigation is not over until the implicated person is allowed the opportunity to offer some facts to support his innocence. It is important to the credibility of the investigations process that the implicated person gets the opportunity to defend himself.

The investigator's goal should be to obtain a confession of wrongdoing from the implicated person. Any reasonable investigator will agree that the confession should be free and voluntary. It should not be obtained through promises, inducements or threats.

Interrogating the Implicated Person

There is a fundamental difference between an interview and an interrogation. The dynamics of the two are completely opposite.

An interview is a non-accusatory fact gathering conversation to determine facts, sequences of events, alibis, or to confirm information with a specific witness. The questions are generally open-ended, and the witness does most of the talking. If close-ended questions are asked, the investigator is usually trying to clearly establish certain facts or to confirm important details. The investigator is not looking for a confession but only for the witness to confirm or deny specific pieces of information.

An interrogation is fundamentally different. It is conducted when the investigator has a valid basis to believe that the implicated person actually committed some wrongdoing. It is a search for admissions and a confession, and these will independently confirm the investigation findings. The admission or confession will also establish the person's participation in the wrongdoing. The investigator is looking for information that establishes the implicated person's culpability and mental state, which are relevant to identifying mitigating circumstance. This information is also relevant later when management determines post-investigation steps like disciplinary action.

Preparing for the Interrogation

An interview of the implicated person must be structured carefully. The purpose of this session is to learn the truth and obtain admissions. Remember that you are not looking for objective information anymore, and the implicated person is not likely to give you additional facts that you can reasonably use.

> **Process Pointer:** In a confrontational interview, keep co-workers and managers outside the room. It is difficult for any implicated person to confess in front of friends or colleagues.
>
> If you think someone else worked with the implicated person in committing the wrongdoing, interview that other person first. This will give you more evidence with which to confront the implicated person.
>
> Before you confront the implicated person, have your documents and statements of others handy to prove up your allegation.
>
> Theme development makes a confession more palatable. The implicated person may have a moral—though not legal—justification for what he did. Morally acceptable themes like financial duress, an intention to pay the money back, poor employer treatment, etc. make it easier for an implicated person to confess.

As you complete your preparation for the interrogation, consider the implicated person's possible motives for committing the wrongdoing. Did he do it for the money? To save his job? To impress someone? When you have some idea—even if it is only a working hypothesis—you can then tailor the interview in that direction.

The theme of this interview should include some explanation as to why an investigation was conducted and what leads you to believe that the person committed the misconduct. It is not necessary to make accusations—in fact, it will probably chill the conversation—but you need the implicated person to understand that you are there for a reason and your interview is not just a "fishing expedition."

You should also clearly state that you are only investigating the allegation and that you have no control over post-investigative steps. This will avoid any claim later on that the implicated person admitted fault only because you said that it would save his job.

> **Process Pointer:** Resist the temptation to bully someone to give you an admission or confession. You will more likely achieve your result if you are friendly and cooperative. People who feel they are being attacked will defensively resist. Get the witness relaxed and talking and see what happens.
>
> Develop the information from the witness before confronting them with any wrongdoing you suspect. Once you confront the witness, you have restricted the flow of facts you are capable of getting.
>
> There is no Fifth Amendment privilege. Employees have no real right to refuse to cooperate and assist the investigation. Also, if an implicated employee claims to be innocent, ask them to point out the proof that shows that. It may speed up your investigations process.
>
> When seeking an admission, you have to be reasonably convinced that the implicated person did the act. You want your interview to distinguish an innocent person from a guilty one. If your goal is to obtain information, then do not use interrogation-style questioning.

Do's and Don'ts of Interrogations

The following is a list of do's and don't that can be helpful to the investigator:

- Do use silence as a weapon. Ask a direct question and wait for a response.
- Do keep questions short.
- Do ask only one question at a time.
- Do question the answers you get.
- Do guard yourself against giving away information.
- Don't make promises of any kind.
- Don't lose your patience or persistence.
- Don't threaten the implicated employee.
- Don't show surprise at any answers.
- Don't use profanity or lower yourself to the level of others.
- Don't be a big shot.
- Don't lie. Whatever you tell must be the truth.
- Don't ever lose your temper. This turns over control to the implicated person, and you will lose the interrogation.
- Don't make excuses for the employee. If you do and it shows up in your documentation, those excuses are likely to be used by the employee for his benefit. Let him make his own excuses.

The person being interrogated is psychologically and emotionally suffering because of your questions. Many wrongdoers want to confess their misconduct. Help him do that.

F. Detecting Insincerity

It is human nature to resist doing something that is uncomfortable. Admitting your wrongdoing to a company investigator when your job may be in jeopardy is one of those things. The greater a person's guilt, the more they will be tempted to deny it or somehow explain it away. They may also try to distance themselves psychologically from the incident.

A key part of interviewing is determining the witness' credibility and the weight to be given to the information offered. You must actively listen.

Listening is much more than just concentrating. Listening skills are learned. They involve perceiving what the witness is actually communicating.

To assess credibility, ask yourself the following questions:

- Was the witness present and aware during the incident?
- How well developed are the witness' powers of observation?
- Is what the witness telling the investigator logical? Does it make sense? Truthful stories are logical. They do not appear to be scripted. Truthful statements are detailed in their presentation of the setting of an event. They reproduce some of the actual conversations, character and mannerisms of the key players in the story.
- What was the witness' demeanor?
- Did the witness make contradictory statements?
- Did the witness have a reason to falsify what was said?
- Does the witness have any known or suspected bias?
- Does the witness stand to gain from the desired outcome?
- What are the witness' relationships to other witnesses and the subject of the investigation?

Also look for the following verbal indicators of deception:

- Attempts to evade questions.
- Vague answers.
- Conflicting information.
- Different answers to the same or similar questions.
- Falsehoods or inaccurate information.

The way in which our bodies show that we are attempting to deceive is referred to as "nonverbal leakage." These are a series of body language clues that indicate insincerity.

An estimated 70 percent of communication is non-verbal. Carefully observe the witness's body posture and physical activity. Everyone uses body language to express themselves. Watch for changes in appearance in response to certain questions. Most people under stress are unaware of their reactions. Use these observations when formulating questions. Look for the following physical indicators of deception:

- *Grooming gestures.* This includes rubbing the hands together, biting fingernails, tapping, swinging, arching the feet, and picking lint or pulling threads off clothes.

- *Eye contact.* Avoiding eye contact conveys nervousness and a lack of confidence.
- *Distance.* Someone who is lying will try to move away from you in order to put more space between you.
- *Behavioral.* Appearing tense, disturbed, excited or agitated.

These manifestations of nervousness may or may not indicate the presence of deception. A good investigator will not base any such conclusion on the observation of just one indicator. Watch for clusters of symptoms, noting where they occur in the interview.

Even an innocent person will feel and exhibit some degree of nervousness in the interview. Look for changes of physical response beyond those manifestations of nervousness the witness displayed when the interview began.

Begin with the presumption that the witness is telling the truth. To begin the interview with a predetermined belief that the witness will be lying is counterproductive to the process. It will likely influence the witness' responses adversely.

Your goal is to obtain as much accurate information as possible. But even false information is useful if you know it is false. It may be easier to terminate an employee for lying during an investigation than it is to prove that they actually committed the misconduct under investigation.

It is important to acknowledge that nearly everyone you interview has his or own agenda or set of objectives (shifting blame, promoting their own interests, or shading the facts in a favorable way, for example). In most instances, it is not hard to see what they are trying to do, and you can discount their information accordingly. In other cases, a process of triangulation will be necessary to tighten down on the true factual picture.

> **Process Pointer:** People lie because they believe that lying will help them more than telling you the truth. You need to convince the witness that telling the truth will be better for him than lying through the interview.
>
> Lying is not a natural human behavior. It has to be done consciously. Consequently, it can be observed. And don't jump to conclusions about the reasons the witness may be lying. Liars have plenty of reasons for what they do.

Truthfulness is signaled by an acute memory, a perceptive recounting of facts, and a flowing narration. Truthful witnesses display a consistent recollection of details and attempt to explain related specifics, often offering more information than they were asked for. They allow the investigator to see their mental wheels turn in search of additional details. They are open and relaxed in their manner of speech, though they may be nervous about the interview. They clearly explain what happened, and they want to be correct.

Deception is the intentional act of concealing or distorting the truth for the purpose of misleading. These witnesses deceive when they deliberately hide from the interviewer what they saw or did, and why they did it.

More than intuition is required to detect deception. A good investigator is familiar with the verbal and non-verbal behaviors that signal deception so they can be noted automatically. The investigator remains alert for inconsistent, evasive responses punctuated by nonverbal signals that show deception. Veracity should be challenged once the investigator has accumulated sufficient data on which to base a proper judgment.

Types of Lies

During an interview, the witness may engage in a variety of different attempts to deceive you. There are five basic types of lies that the witness may use.

The first type of lie is the simple denial. Its simplicity might lead you to think that this type would be chosen often. But many people avoid denying the incident directly. Psychologists call this "cognitive dissonance." To avoid this, the witness will likely go to great lengths to avoid having to deny it directly.

The second type of lie is the lie of omission. This is the most common type. It is the simplest lie because the witness merely tells the truth but leaves out the information that could be embarrassing or incriminating. Because the remaining part of the witness' statement is true, it can be repeated consistently. If the witness is presented with the omitted information, he can just say he forgot to mention it. A lie of omission can only succeed if the investigator is not prepared to force the subject by mentioning the excluded information.

The third type is the lie of fabrication. This is the most difficult type of lie because it requires the witness to be inventive and have a good memory so that the lie remains consistent. This type of lie also creates the most stress for the witness.

An investigator should ask questions when this type is suspected that show that the explanation does not hold up to specific questioning. If the investigation can disprove the witness' sequence of events or details it may prove as damning as a confession of wrongdoing.

The fourth type of lie is minimization. Here, the witness offers a small admission of fault hoping that the investigator will be satisfied and discontinue any further questioning. When this type of lie is used, it is a strong indication that additional information is being withheld.

The final type of lie is the lie of exaggeration. A witness may exaggerate the actions of another person or an aspect of a particular conversation. The lie may be used by someone who wants to increase the value of their information or inflate their own importance. If the investigator maintains a healthy skepticism and questions each claim, the investigator should be able to identify any contractions.

Lies told in an interview can be as powerful as a confession. Lying in a workplace investigation likely exposes the employee to disciplinary action. An investigator must constantly be aware of the possibility that the subject is withholding information or intentionally attempting to deceive.

G. The Interview Memo

If you are going to rely on any of the information from the interview, then you must memorialize the witness' statements. Just as a relevant document taken from a filing cabinet serves as a component for your findings, so should a memorandum of the interview. When prepared correctly, it stands as a separate piece of investigation evidence.

> **Process Pointer:** A good memo can protect you later on if the witness denies something or accuses you of an improper line of questioning. Get in the habit of writing complete memos that can stand on their own.

Resist the temptation to simply drop your handwritten notes in the file. Your notes are your subjective understanding of the matters discussed. It will also be written in your unique shorthand. The risk is that others may review these notes and draw different conclusions from your notes. Worse, you may be asked to recall things that happened and not be able to decipher what you wrote. If another person is taking notes, then the risks are compounded, especially the risk that the two sets of notes contradicts each other in some way. Either way, your investigation is, practically speaking, deprived of the precise information the witness offered. You have inadvertently inserted yourself into the investigation process by now having to act as some kind of interpreter to explain what the witness said. Stated another way, the value of this witness now depends not on what he said, but rather on what you recall that they said. You are, essentially, now the witness to hearsay information.

Instead, as soon as possible after the interview is completed, draft a simple memo to the file transcribing your notes into simple declarative sentences or a narrative of the conversation. Use as many direct quotes as possible. Then destroy your handwritten notes. The memo should be the sole written recollection of the interview. Through this process, you will identify any gaps in your questioning that will require you to get supplemental information from the witness. You are also more likely to remember details that you left out of your notes but should be added to the memo. If for some reason you cannot decipher your notes, you will then be able to expeditiously correct the situation.

Some may ask whether the witness should review the memo or sign it to signify that they agree to its accuracy. This should not be done. The memo represents the trained investigator's recording of information gathered from the witness. It does not represent the collaborative process of the witness and the investigator. The information, if properly gathered, stands on its own even without the agreement of the witness because, presumably, he said those words. There is also a practical problem with seeking the agreement of the witness. What will you do if the witness disagrees—as opposed to supplementing or clarifying a statement—that he said something that the investigator recalled? How will you reconcile the disagreement? The practical effect of the disagreement will be to undermine the value of that memo by your self-defeating attempt to underscore the fairness of the process.

One word of caution: make the memo a good one. If there is a lawsuit, a complaint to a regulatory agency or even an internal inquiry, the memo is going to be produced. If the witness is key to your investigation findings, any scrutiny of your conclusions will include a scrutiny of that memo. Remember that the memo can be both a sword and a shield. A properly documented interview memo not only will justify a management decision but it can also protect you from a claim that the findings were unsupported or the implicated employee did not admit what he actually admitted to you. It can also prove a negative. For example, if a witness falsely claims that he said something in the interview that somehow favors their position, its omission from a proper, contemporaneously prepared interview memo is going to show that it is more likely than not that the statement was not made.

> **Process Pointer:** Although reasonable people may disagree, interview notes should be destroyed after you prepare the interview memorandum. This ensures that there is only one statement prepared regarding what happened in the interview. However, make sure that the memorandum is as complete as your notes.
>
> Do not write your interview memo in question-and-answer format. It makes reading it tedious, and you could be challenged as to why you asked a particular question and not another.
>
> The interview memo is the heart of the investigation report. Always write a separate one for each witness.
>
> The interview memo should have clear and concise evidence. Write like you speak. Avoid using the third person to describe the interviewer. And don't use stilted or pretentious wording.

H. Interview Problems

Despite your best preparation, you cannot prevent problems. But you can be ready for them.

Requesting a Lawyer

A witness may ask if he needs a lawyer. This poses a problem that requires an immediate response. While everyone has the right to consult an attorney, your company has the right to require its employees to disclose information that they have that related to the company's business. The conventional wisdom is to reply that only the witness should make that decision. Offer no opinion on whether the witness needs a lawyer. If you are an attorney, repeat that you are representing the company and cannot provide the witness with any legal advice. Your notes should state the substance of this exchange during the interview. Management is not required to allow interview subjects to have a lawyer and can insist that the interview continue with the witness without a lawyer present. The company is entitled to one-on-one communications with its employees, and not ones that are filtered through attorneys or made more difficult by the legal adversary process.

Sometimes you may choose to allow the witness to bring an attorney. This usually happens when you want the witness' information more than you want to fight about a lawyer being present. If so, you must not let the attorney take over the interview or disrupt it in any way. Instead, give them a full opportunity at the end of the interview to state their position.

Refusing the Interview

An employee may state that he does not want to be interviewed. This problem should be addressed earlier as a matter of company policy. Your company should articulate to its employees that the company has a "talk or walk" policy, meaning that employees must cooperate with a workplace investigation or risk losing their jobs.

While it is generally true that an employee has a duty to cooperate with the investigation, you must never appear to bully the employee into agreeing to the interview. If the interview is essential, your company may very well conclude that it is appropriate to bring disciplinary proceedings against the employee for refusing to cooperate with the investigation.

Employees may have a Fifth Amendment right under the U.S. Constitution not to make self-incriminating statements to the government. They have no equivalent right to refuse to make a statement to their employer, and certainly no constitutional right to keep a job with the company after refusing to talk with company representatives.

However, as with any employee termination related to the investigation, the company should determine, before terminating an employee for not cooperating with the investigation, whether that termination would harm the company's own interests. After all, an employee cannot be expected to cooperate with the company's investigation after being terminated.

> **Process Pointer:** Although an employer may fire someone who refuses to cooperate with the investigation, a termination is not going to get you the information you need. Consider the reasons why the person is reluctant to speak with you and see if those concerns can be accommodated. If the employee outright refuses, develop another investigative strategy. The strategy should consider whether the employee has guilty knowledge that he is trying to keep from you.

Placing Conditions on the Interview

An employee may also insist that an interview take place under certain conditions. These conditions might include (i) the participation of the employee's lawyer; (ii) the tape-recording of the interview; (iii) that certain topics will not be discussed; or (iv) that the company will not disclose certain parts of the interview without that employee's prior consent. This situation requires both you and management to weigh the need for the information against the burdens imposed if the company agrees. If the company agrees, the agreement should be in writing. The company should also consider the extent to which applicable legal privileges against disclosure might be deemed to be waived.

At the beginning of an investigation and at various points during its course, you should make a good-faith assessment whether the matter under investigation poses the risk of criminal liability for the company or any of the employees. If so, you should inform the witness of the option to retain personal counsel and have the personal counsel present during the interview. If requested, be prepared to postpone or suspend the interview long enough to permit the witness to obtain counsel or consider whether to do so.

> **Process Pointer:** When the witness becomes difficult with you, resist the temptation to strong-arm his participation. The success of your interview depends on his willingness to give you information. Don't react to witness' statements and try to disarm them. Change your approach. And remember that witnesses resist for a variety of reasons and not just to conceal misconduct.

I. Collection and Review of Documents

Documents form the foundation of most investigations. Documents frequently identify information that helps prove the wrongdoing. Important information can be found in a variety of document types, including computer records, internal memos, transactional documents, financial records, expense account reports and phone logs.

Documents often provide the best record of the conduct under investigation. Documents generally fall into two categories: paper and electronic. You generally take the lead in document gathering and examination. The process must be thorough and well documented.

Witnesses may be reluctant to supply information voluntarily, especially when it may implicate their own actions or the actions of those they supervise or with whom they work. Similarly, witness recollections of events often fade with time and may be inconsistent with recollections of other witnesses. Documents are essential in the process of refreshing a witness' memory and might also help the investigator reconcile conflicting recollections. Documents can also help determine or assess a person's intent or motive in doing something. Documents often provide the best record of the conduct at issue.

E-mails are especially useful. Instantaneous screen edits and a "point, click, send" culture have eliminated the time delay that used to allow cooler heads to prevail when sending intemperate notes. The prevalence of electronic messages has created a false sense of security in many employees and lulled them into making exchanges of information that they never would do face-to-face. Consequently, an e-mail message may give you valuable insight into the real dynamics that were going on at that moment in time, rather than the careful descriptions of events you might hear in an interview.

Be careful to identify all relevant documents. The search should also include informal as well as formal company records. In many companies, for example, employees maintain their own personal desk files in addition to the official company files. These need to be included in the search. Where appropriate, review the implicated person's personnel file. The file may reveal other symptoms consistent with the report. But don't overdo it either. An investigation differs from litigation, where lawyers seek every possible shred of paper. You want only the relevant documents. Your goal is to substantiate an allegation of actual or suspected wrongdoing.

The files of potential wrongdoers should be reviewed and all documents appropriate to a particular investigation should be examined, including such items as calendars, letters, e-mails, voicemail messages, expense reports, etc. If there is a concern that an employee may try to hide or destroy files, consider obtaining them without first requesting them from the employee, and perhaps without the employee's knowledge.

The gathering of electronic documents, including e-mails, information stored on networks, diskettes, back-up tapes and personal computers, requires special attention. Best practices for the handling of electronic evidence change constantly. Computers frequently contain smoking-gun evidence.

When needed, meet with appropriate information technology personnel to ensure that all potentially relevant sources have been searched. You will need to know (i) the type and model of the computer used, (ii) the capacity of the internal hard disk and the external disk drives; (iii) the operating system; (iv) the applications used on the computer and where they are stored, and (v) the computer literacy of the implicated person. Electronic document searches frequently result in the recovery of too much data. Using selective word searches, the investigator can filter large amounts of records and data into manageable amounts.

When handling investigation documents, take certain precautions. Documents should be indexed so they can be found when needed. Original documents should not be marked or altered in any way. There may be multiple copies of some documents. Retain these copies, especially if they include important margin notes or other markings. It may become important to know which individuals maintained a copy in their files. Compare versions of what appears to be the same document for alterations.

An original document is you received from someone else, even if it is a copy. It does not include any copies you made. If you need a working copy of the document, copy the original. Put the original in the file, and mark the copies up as needed. Following this practice will prevent an inadvertent alteration of original documents and ensure that these documents will not be invalidated or challenged later as a result of the your markings.

The authenticity of documents becomes critical in investigations where document tampering is suspected. Therefore, in some instances it may become necessary to obtain the same documents from more than one independent source. Indicate which copy of the document came from which source.

The documents should be included as part of the investigation file. The file should contain each of the following documents:

- Correspondence.
- The investigation plan.
- Interview memoranda.
- Notes on discussions with attorneys, Human Resources, auditors and other professionals about the investigation.
- Copies of relevant fact-related documents.

Treat the file as confidential and store it in a locked cabinet. Only those persons with a need to know should be given access to the files. Once the investigation is complete, the files should be stored so that the confidentiality of the information is maintained. Ensure that their files of closed investigations are stored safely and for as long as your company's document retention guidelines require.

Be observant about the details regarding the substance as well as the context and circumstances in which documents are prepared and maintained. Additionally, be alert to alterations, white-out areas, erased margin notes, earlier drafts and documents that should be present but are missing.

> **Process Pointer:** Interviews and document-gathering are only means to an end. The purpose is to give the investigator the information he needs to confront the implicated person and obtain an admission of wrongdoing.
>
> Don't slow the process down by trying to get every possible document that might be relevant. Just consider the scope of the investigation and the facts you need to prove. Then ask yourself what documents cover those areas.

J. Management Steps

No matter how good the investigator or the investigation, the objective of the investigation is to present information to management to enable them to make the necessary decisions for the benefit of the company and its shareholders. To accomplish this, the findings must be placed in a written report which is sufficient to inform management of the relevant facts and at the same time lay the groundwork for compliance business improvement, the commencement of civil litigation and/or a referral of the matter to law enforcement. This is important to investigations. A useful report highlights your value and underscores your importance to the company.

Reporting the Findings

Sometimes, business managers would rather not see anything in writing. This view should be unacceptable to executive management and certainly to you. There are a variety of methods available to the corporation through legal counsel to assure a limited distribution of an investigative report. The first time an investigative report is suppressed for the purpose of avoiding a proper review by management marks the beginning of the end of compliance investigative integrity for the company.

The outcome of the investigation must provide answers to the "magic questions" of the investigation: who, what, where, when, why and how. The detail provided should be sufficient to explain compliance business processes to someone who is unfamiliar with the business. If you accurately tell the story in the fewest words, you stand a better chance of having the report reviewed.

As companies increasingly view you as business counselors, reporting the findings is the best opportunity to the value of the workplace investigations unit to your company. You need good communications abilities, problem-solving skills, knowledge of the business and client-partnership skills.

The Final Report

If your investigation is part of a business process, the final report is your finished product. It is the sum total of your efforts and proof-positive that an investigation was conducted. A well-written report shows that you have done your job and that you recognize your responsibilities to the company.

> **Process Pointer:** Writing final reports is not easy. But they represent a critical element of a good investigation. It gives your investigation credibility. If it is poor, you risk ruining an otherwise good investigation.
>
> Let someone else draw the conclusions. You are just a presenter of facts. If you are tempted to offer a conclusion or opinion, it is probably because your final report is not clear enough, and you are trying to help the reader along.

A written report creates a lasting record of the findings and allows management to consider its contents over time. A written report is a persuasive way of communicating that misconduct did (or did not) occur or that corrective action has already been taken. The report also provides support for the company's ultimate decision in resolving the matter, and it shows that the company's investigative process was objective and neutral. Finally, the report constitutes the company's "stake in the ground;" the company has committed to these facts when making its decision regarding how to proceed. A template of a Final Report may be found in Appendix O.

When conducting any investigation, you must accept the fact that some fundamental questions may never be known for a fact. When investigating fraud and misconduct, there is no DNA or fingerprints to give you certainty. You will just never find that kind of proof. You have to rely on testimony, documents, corroboration and credibility. If you do your job, you may not know everything, but everything you know will add up.

The form of the report depends on its intended use. The Final Report is not a chronology of the investigation. It is not a stream-of-consciousness recitation of every fact elicited. The report states whether the allegations of misconduct were substantiated, unsubstantiated, or whether the findings were inconclusive. If the report is substantiated, the Final Report will cite the policies violated and the harm the company suffered as a result. If the employee admits wrongdoing or resigns before the Final Report is issued, the report will include that information as well.

The Final Report is limited by the scope of the investigation. The scope should also be clearly specified in the report. The report's recommendations and findings should be limited by that scope as well. This will provide a clear understanding to anyone to whom the report is disclosed regarding the investigation's limitations. Later on, as additional facts develop, you may need to explain why the findings did not cover the areas under scrutiny. Without a scope specified, your investigation may look incomplete or incompetent.

Once the investigation is concluded, you are ready to draft the Final Report. The report includes:

- The nature of the report and how it brought to your attention;
- A summary of the facts gathered throughout the investigation, including a chronology of events. This is a neutral narrative of the key events uncovered by the investigation;
- The people interviewed and the documents reviewed;
- A brief discussion of any credibility assessments reached;
- What created the opportunity, and how much opportunity did the subject have;

- Whether the report was substantiated or unsubstantiated or the results were inconclusive. If substantiated, what conclusions are supported by what was found;
- The specific conclusion(s) reached on each key issue;
- The identification of any issues that could not be resolved in the investigation;
- A brief discussion of how the company guidelines or policies apply to the situation;
- Whether applicable controls were adequate or circumvented;
- Whether any relevant compliance controls were followed to prevent other problems or reduce the impact;
- How long has the problem gone on, and what, if any, is the financial impact to the company or third parties;
- How is the company responding to the report, if it is substantiated; and
- A list of the key documents used in the investigation.

> **Process Pointer:** You must compile the facts into a theory about what happened and tell a story. Facts alone prove little. The mathematician Henri Poincare once said: "Science is built up with facts, as a house is with stones. But a collection of facts is no more a science than a heap of stones is a house."

A proper Final Report offers no recommendations on how an offending employee should be disciplined, whether the company should compensate someone, or similar possible post-investigation actions. Those steps are outside the scope of the investigation. Also, if you can decide on the resulting disciplinary action to be taken, a conflict of interest may be created that interferes with your ability to find the objective truth of what happened. However, the Final Report may include recommendations for additional investigation and corrective changes to the business' operations.

Regardless of the format you choose, there are some basic considerations to ensure the content of the report is helpful. Keep it simple and factual. Facts make up the backbone of all reports.

Use the first person singular when referring to yourself. Using the third person is awkward and should be avoided. Be direct in your explanations.

Strive for clarity and accuracy. Words create expectations that add to or detract from any writing. Appreciate the implications of your words and how they could be unintentionally misconstrued. Remember that words carry many meanings.

The report should never contain the investigator's opinions. It should not state, for example, that "John Smith appeared uninterested." Rather, it should state that "John Smith continually looked around the room and requested that questions be repeated to him two or three times before he would answer."

The report must explicitly and precisely describe any documents which are part of the findings. Do not use phrases like "the records include the following . . ." because that implies that there are other records besides the ones mentioned.

The report must reach conclusions, even when it might seem difficult to do so. Assess the credibility of the witnesses. Examine the objective facts and consider motivations. State each of these factors clearly and explicitly. However, do not use emphasis—such as, "the manager was thoroughly incompetent"—when expressing findings or conclusions.

Factual assumptions should be described specifically and in detail. There should be no guessing regarding the factual assumptions upon which a finding is based. Avoid terms like "supposedly" and "presumably."

The report should use direct quotes whenever possible. Quoting a witness directly strengthens the factual assertions.

Be careful when using pronouns. Be clear to be sure to whom they refer.

When possible, the report should refer to relevant company policies, practices and written procedures. This grounds the factual context within the operations of the business.

Avoid expressing opinions because opinions can easily be challenged. Once doubt is brought to opinions expressed in the report, the credibility of the report, report and investigation may also be challenged. It is better to focus on what the facts show, rather than what the investigator personally concludes from the inquiries.

Avoid inflammatory or judgmental words. The report is intended to gather facts only, not pass judgments on others.

Stick to company business. The scope of the report should be focused on the specific issues under investigation.

Your tone should be respectful, courteous and constructive, even if you think that a witness was lying to you or the proven misconduct was egregious.

The report should be written as if the report will be published. It might be included in documents that are more widely circulated.

Do not make legal conclusions about any perceived law violations, breaches of contract, or potential corporate liability. These conclusions are outside the scope of the investigation. You may also not have the competence to make those conclusions.

Do not include any of your observations or similar conclusions that could be construed as admissions of company liability. If a witness makes a statement that could be construed as such, and you believe that the statement should be included, be sure to attribute the statement clearly: "John Smith stated in his interview that he believed that this violated the law."

The report should specify any contradictions which surfaced during the interview. Contradictions can exist between documents and interviews, among different witnesses or when the witness contradicts himself. Indicate whether, through your efforts, you were able to resolve any conflicts in testimony or documents. Otherwise, unresolved contradictions may reflect negatively on your investigation.

If an acknowledgement, admission or confession is made, be specific as to exactly what was admitted. If the individual acknowledged doing two things, the investigator should write out exactly what happened so that a reader cannot possibly incorrectly believe that he admitted to doing ten or only one.

The report should not report the investigator's conclusions about the merits of the allegations or offer an opinion on what, if any, action should be taken regarding the subject of the investigation or a witness.

Be brief, but tell a complete story. Write for an educated audience, but not someone who is knowledgeable about that part of the business. Define all technical terms, jargon and acronyms. (The Final Report may, after all, end up distributed outside your company.)

The ultimate test of a good Final Report is simply this: if the reader of the report has a question, the report is deficient.

> **Process Pointer:** Do not make recommendations regarding disciplinary action. This creates a conflict of interest because it will create the appearance that you tailored your findings to support your recommendation. Offer the findings and let others decide what to do with them.
>
> Use care when communicating the results of an investigation. Be certain that the person who asks for it has a justifiable business purpose for knowing the information. The company can be liable for over-disseminating the investigation results.
>
> Never put your opinions in the final report. If doubt is later cast on the validity of your opinion, then that doubt will undermine the credibility of your report and the underlying investigation. Focus instead on what the facts show, rather than your own personal insights, however valid and accurate they might be.

The drafting of the Final Report, however, is not without risks. Think before writing. If the report will cover any sensitive areas, consult the company's legal department first. At least in the most sensitive areas, and in any preparation for litigation, the company may take steps to permit it to assert the attorney-client and other privileges. But remember that this is a business process. These risks must also be balanced against the benefits to the business if a detailed report leads to corrective steps.

Great care should be taken to protect the confidentiality of the final report. A written report means there is a greater risk of disclosure to people who should not read the report. Given the ubiquity of photocopiers, scanners and e-mail, it is easy to copy and circulate a report widely.

Other Investigation Reports

You may not just write the final report as part of your investigation process. You may also write other types of reports.

An initial report may be written shortly after the investigation is opened. It describes the progress of the investigation and details the leads to be followed.

If an investigation lasts for an extended period of time, you may write a progress report. Progress reports of the investigation are written at fixed intervals to detail the progress of the investigation. Progress reports in some form are usually prepared every 30 days or so.

If something unusual occurs, you might prepare a special report. This can be a supplement to a progress report, but it must be able to stand separately form the progress report. An example of such a report may be a specific meeting or surveillance.

Action in Light of the Investigation

The final step in the investigation process is for the company to implement corrective action. Ensure that management has met with the person who was the subject of the investigation as well as the employee who raised the issue.

Remedial action must be proper and prompt. Internal remedial steps could include revising corporate procedures or management structures, revising compliance procedures or oversight, as well as employee disciplinary action. It might also include specifying best practices and increasing employee training. External remedial steps could include disclosures in public filings and compensating injured third parties.

The Final Report will also facilitate everyone's attention and agreement regarding the substantiated problem. The discovered problem may trigger an audit to prevent future and more serious problems.

The Final Report may have collateral value to the company. If the report is used in a private litigation, the findings can defend the company from certain claims. Because the report will contain specific findings of fact and the bases for the findings, the report can be used as a guide to resolve the dispute informally. These uses, however, must be balanced against the risks of waiving applicable legal privileges, identifying wrongdoers and the sources of information, and the possibility that the report may be circulated beyond the company's control.

If the misconduct—or the perception of misconduct that was actually proper behavior—was seen to have impacted a wider group of people, such as the implicated employee's department, a manager may want to debrief the work group. The debriefing could take the form of bringing all employees together at the same time in a meeting format. This lets everyone have the same information about the allegations, the scope and results of the investigation, and what, if any, changes may be made in the workplace. Debriefing meetings can be an effective method for neutralizing rumors and miscommunications among employees. They also provide the opportunity to reinforce company policies and management directives.

After the meeting, and in those circumstances where appropriate, managers should send the affected staff a memo reminding them about your company's policy against retaliation. A sample memo may be found in Appendix O.

K. Tracking and Metrics

You are delivering value to the company. Remember that client satisfaction depends on properly managing their expectations. That means describing and supporting how your investigations are helping to improve the business.

The measurement of quality and productivity is an essential component of managing investigations as an embedded business process. Find ways to measure the values of the investigative process in terms which have a relevance to those values which contribute to the company's profits. Few senior managers will fund an investigative process without strong proof that a contribution to the bottom line will result.

Your audience for receiving metrics can be wide or narrow. Recipients may include the board of directors (or just the audit committee), the legal department, the chief compliance officer, executive management and/or business unit managers.

When you fail to measure their value to the business enterprise, you give management the opportunity to view the function as just one more expense of the business and not as a contributor to company value. Some may consider it easier and less expensive to avoid misconduct investigations and to simply terminate the employee or pay the employee a healthy severance to simply go away. Although it is an expensive decision for a company to proceed this way, without metrics there is no way to show the true costs of that decision. Measuring the investigative function and its ability to productively conduct investigations and offer decision-making support to management can be shown to make a productive contribution to company equity and long-term loyalty.

Because it's also a process, show that the investigations are an effective business function. Therefore, provide senior managers and/or the board of directors with an overview of investigations opened during a specified time period, usually a month or a calendar quarter. Background information tracked by the compliance group and reported generally includes:

- The date the investigation was opened.
- The date the investigation was closed.
- The name and location of the reporter, if known.
- The name of the individual responsible for the resolution of the complaint.
- The nature of the complaint (i.e. the issue type).
- A summary of the facts elicited by the investigation, including whether the allegations were substantiated.
- The disciplinary or remedial action taken, if necessary.

There are a variety of metrics to measure the investigative process, and the most relevant focus on the efficacy of the process. Consider any of these measurements:

- Number of incidents reported per 1000 employees.
- Percentage of employees disciplined for misconduct.
- Percentage of total compliance failures detected internally.
- Percentage of total compliance failures detected by hotline call.
- Percentage of total allegations that are substantiated.
- Percentage of contacts to the compliance and ethics office reporting an allegation.
- Percentage of contacts to the compliance and ethics office seeking advice.
- Summary (and corresponding percentage) of most frequent allegations.
- Investigation cycle time during a specific time period.
- Number of cases opened during a specific time period.
- Number of cases closed during a specific time period.
- Average cost to conduct an investigation during a specific time period
- Summary of substantiated cases (including root causes and recommendations) during a specific time period.

To overcome the misconceptions of managers as to the purpose of the compliance investigative function, talk in terms these managers understand. Communicate results that contribute to the company's profits and well-being. Look for ways to present meaningful data which reflects its achievements and essential role as an embedded business function within the operations of the company.

L. Executive Summaries

Investigations defy easy quantification. Don't place too much stock in the persuasive effect of your statistics. As to a specific case, these decision-makers are not likely to focus on a specific investigation of yours unless it is a significant one. But it is important to cultivate these people as your allies. After all, your investigations protect their interests.

A simple way to show them your value is to send a monthly executive summary to key business leaders in your company. The summary should include a status report on each investigation that remains pending as of the date of your summary. Mention what you have uncovered so far, and state your overall objective for the investigation. Objectives include identifying contributory fault by third-parties, as well as identifying process deficiencies. Remind them indirectly that substantiating the misconduct is just one part of what you are doing.

Give a full summary of any closed investigations. This would include substantiated cases, unsubstantiated cases, and inconclusive ones. State your findings and whether other departments assisted the investigation. If there were breakdowns in the process, say so. State any "lessons learned" in order to underscore the investigation's relevance to the business. If you expect any future steps to be taken, such as a referral to law enforcement, be sure to mention it.

M. Business Ethics Bulletins

Another way to increase your visibility is to disseminate information about specific investigations that yielded important operational information. By showcasing compliance violation cases and subsequent penalties, you are highlighting the company's commitment to ethical standards and necessary corrective action. The perception that the company is committed enhances employee belief in ethics messages.

Ethics bulletins serve as awareness and education tools by providing real-world examples of corporate violations. These examples resonate more fully with employees than hypothetical, abstract training examples. For example, some investigations identify specific procedural flaws—unsecured company property, insufficient safeguards on sensitive information, unsupervised employees—that are likely to be recurring elsewhere. Using the investigation's factual findings (or a sterilized version of them) can give the readers a practical example of what happened and what they need to do to prevent it from happening to them. It will make the information more meaningful than just an abstract admonition to be careful. A sample bulletin may be found in Appendix Q.

Your business ethics bulletins should follow each of these principles:

- The bulletin should be clear, concise and easy to read.
- The bulletin should never identify involved employees by name.
- The bulletin should state how the activity was uncovered.
- The bulletin should relate specific facts regarding the activity or offense to help prevent future occurrences of a similar nature.
- The bulletin should give relevant and specific facts regarding the investigation.
- The bulletin should emphasize the importance of adhering to the company's code of conduct regardless of the amount at issue (if the offense appears to be of a small dollar amount).
- The bulleting should mention any instances of reluctant or refused cooperation with investigators in order to stress the importance of full cooperation.
- The bulletin should state the specific policy violated and the result.
- The bulletin's key takeaways section should be as concrete and specific as possible.

An added benefit of the bulletins is that it reminds your colleagues in the other departments that you exist for more than just answering calls to the whistleblower hotline. Increased visibility may also encourage them to alert you directly in the future.

> **Process Pointer:** The process requires you to prepare the final report, but other documents such as summaries and bulletins help convey the information so that it can be used by your business colleagues to improve operations. Think about how your information can be most effectively presented. After all, if the information is not conveyed in an effective way, your process will also be seen as ineffective.

N. Reporting to the Reporter

When the investigation is complete, you need to inform the reporter accordingly. In some cases, the reporter will be an employee of your company, but the reporter may also be an outsider. Either way, you need to be able to explain that the investigation was completed in a commercially reasonable way, and that the process is done. Unless you respond, the perception will be that the initial report was not investigated, and that it fell down some black hole in the corporate bureaucracy. A response closes the process, reinforces its fairness, and it may anticipate (or preempt) the contact by a dissatisfied reporter to your executive management, a regulator or the media.

However, you must remember not to breach your confidentiality obligations, and you should not disclose anything that could be construed as your (inadvertent) admission of company liability. The easiest approach is usually (i) to thank the reporter for reporting the matter to you; (ii) to tell them that the investigation is now complete; and (iii) that any corrective action, if necessary, will be promptly taken. Don't disclose whether the allegation was substantiated or what disciplinary action may be taken against employees. The reporter only has a reasonable expectation to be informed that their concerns were handled appropriately. A sample response to the reporter may be found in Appendix R.

PART IV

Other Investigation Issues

A. Operational Security

Operational security (known in military circles as "OPSEC") is a methodology that denied critical information to an adversary. OPSEC protects information that is associated with sensitive operations and activities. OPSEC is generally regarded not only as a methodology, but also a mindset. Make sure you consider the OPSEC of your investigations.

Protect the investigation's integrity

In the classic movie "The Godfather," there is a scene where the heads of the Corleone family are meeting with another gangster who has a business proposition for them to consider. Everyone maintains a stony silence, except for Santino, the hot-headed son who interrupts his father by commenting on the proposition. After the meeting, Don Corleone upbraids his son: "Never tell anyone outside the family what you are thinking." Therein lies a cautionary lesson for investigators as well as mobsters.

During your investigation, you may be developing a good sense about who is implicated in the misconduct. But do you know for sure? Could a business person who is assisting you with the investigation be involved? A cooperating employee may not even be complicit in the wrongdoing; he may just be acting irresponsibly. It may be someone who is so enthusiastic about assisting you that he goes too far. He may be someone who empathizes with the implicated employees—for instance, he doesn't want someone to go to jail and lose custody of their children—that his seemingly innocent contacts with them have the unintended effect of tipping them off to your investigation.

The lesson is this: keep everyone other than your investigative team on a "need to know" basis. Don't share your hypothesis, strategy, tentative conclusions, concerns, etc. If the integrity of the investigation is compromised, it may be impossible to rehabilitate it. This would be all the more unfortunate because your compromising disclosures were not necessary for your investigation to succeed.

Control, control, control

Someone has to control the investigation. It had better be you. Any good investigator will coordinate his investigation with his business-unit clients. After all, they are the ones who assist the investigator and the investigator, in return, tries to make the investigation relevant to the needs of the business. But you must never investigate by committee.

So maintain exclusive control. Dictate the steps to be taken, and the proof that needs to be gathered. While everyone wants to have business people engaged in the process, their role is a limited one. You are the one who is singularly responsible to your company for the quality of investigation. No investigator should ever compromise standards—in timing, proof needed, people interviewed, etc.—simply because senior managers are clamoring for quick action. Stand your ground. If they are truly professional, then they will respect your prerogative and follow your lead.

Interim Measures

When serious allegations of misconduct are directed toward a particular employee, the company must immediately react. There may be a need for preliminary action pending the completion of your investigation. If necessary to protect the health and safety of any employee or to protect the integrity of the company's policies and procedures, or even the need to simply "stop the action" until the investigation can be completed, management may consider taking any of the following steps:

- Suspension of the alleged offender, with or without pay.
- Sending the employee home without a suspension, but on a paid leave of absence until the matter can be reviewed.
- Temporary transfer of an employee pending the completion of the investigation.

Suspending or terminating an employee severely limits the investigator's ability to confront the employee under conditions carefully designed and structured to maximize the likelihood of a confession. In other words, try to control the environment in which the interview is to take place. The element of surprise may be critical, as the employee will not have had an opportunity to plan and rehearse an explanation for the conduct. Moreover, the interviewer will be able to gauge the employee's reaction to particular questions, and the interviewer will be prepared to present contradictory evidence if needed.

If the employee is alerted to the allegation, which is inevitable if her or she is suspended or terminated before you can interview them, the likelihood of a successful confrontation is diminished, especially if the employee retains a lawyer. Proactive measures to obtain damaging evidence against the employee through surveillance or similar measures will, in all likelihood, be lost. The employee may also try to influence other witnesses or third parties who know of the misconduct, or the employee may try to destroy relevant documents or other evidence.

You must recognize that there will be circumstances where the company will have no choice but to suspend or terminate the employee. However, in the absence of a genuine threat to the company's financial well-being, the better choice is to wait until the confrontational interview with the subject has taken place. Whatever the choice, interim steps must be coordinated between the investigative team and executive management.

There are other ways to "stop the action." Cut off the implicated employee's access to the email server and other computer systems. Then capture past messages from the server to assist your case. Cancel access cards to your company offices. Retrieve employee identification cards.

The investigation process requires you to catch up on facts that have already happened. Do your best to keep from having to catch up with facts as they continue to happen.

> **Process Pointer:** Be creative with interim measures. An employee has no right to continue working unaffected by the investigation. It is only wrong to penalize them if the investigation has not been completed. This might seem unfair in some way, but investigations are one of the realities of being a corporate employee.

B. Special Concerns of Investigations

The overriding principle involved in conducting workplace investigations is "do no harm." Bad situations in companies have been made worse by poor investigations that look incompetent at best and as cover-ups at worst.

Workplace investigations carry inherent risks. The workplace investigations unit must be mindful of possible tort claims arising from how the investigation is conducted, regardless of its outcome.

Unethical Investigator Behavior

A reputation for unethical behavior by investigators undermines any value that the workplace investigations unit brings to the company. It damages the quality of investigations as well as the respect the unit enjoys within the company. Any of the following behaviors are unacceptable for investigators:

- Selectively opening, closing, rushing or stalling an investigation based on a relationship with a victim, implicated person, witness or executive.
- Improperly handling evidence to influence the outcome of an investigation.
- Improperly handling evidence or testimony through incompetence.
- Fabricating information.
- Using interrogation tactics instead of interviewing tactics.
- Treating each witness as though culpable, with little or no regard for the damage inflicted on blameless people.
- Making inappropriate threats or promises to employees.
- Compromising sensitive information or disclosing it improperly.
- Mistreating liaison contacts.

Unethical behavior exposes the company to civil and criminal liability. Make ethics a pillar of your operations.

Opening Pandora's Box

When a company is a victim of employee misconduct, and when that misconduct becomes public, the company faces harm beyond its immediate losses. For example, an investigation can be so effective in discovering misconduct that it develops information that would never have been learned by government or private litigants. The investigation process may also encourage disgruntled employees to make accusations that otherwise would not be disclosed. The investigation may disrupt company operations. Finally, the investigation may create adverse publicity and create internal divisiveness by employees who are being asked to report on the activities of others in their workplace.

Common Investigator Errors

There is no single way to conduct a proper investigation. Methods vary depending on investigators and investigations. Despite differing methods, some common problems may arise:

Promptness. Companies may wait too long to investigate. This may result from delays in contacting reporters, referring the matter to investigators or delays in management reporting the matter to you. Delays compromise witness recollections and other proof.

Impartiality. Companies may use an investigator who is somehow vested in the outcome of the investigation. This could be an investigator who is connected to the incidents under investigation. It could be an investigator who is in the management hierarchy for that business unit. You may not be neutral in the outcome of the investigation. If your neutrality is compromised, so is the investigation. Even an investigation conducted to "clear" a subject may be compromised by an investigation's bias to reach a particular finding.

Confidentiality. You must maintain confidentiality of the subject and the witnesses. This must be balanced against the need to conduct a thorough investigation and to afford the subject a full opportunity to respond. The investigator must be sure that the investigation is not compromised by witnesses talking to or trying to influence others.

Training. A common error is the use of untrained—or under-trained—investigators. Do choose someone who has little understanding of the substantive issues and no training or experience in conducting investigations and making credibility determinations.

Thoroughness. Inexperienced investigators have trouble understanding who they should interview, and in what order. They also frequently do not know how far to go. Their investigations may be merely superficial, with few witnesses interviewed and no real attempt to determine the facts. Conversely, they may wish to talk to every witness who has been mentioned in the investigation.

Questioning. This is a difficult part of the investigation process. Some investigators may ask questions that are too narrow. There is nothing wrong with asking narrow questions, but narrow questions elicit a different response than open-ended questions. Poorly trained investigators may ask few questions. They may simply ask the reporter to tell his or her side of the story, and then they may do the same with the subject of the investigation. These investigators usually do not understand the law and the fact issues.

Determining Credibility. Untrained investigators frequently are unable to determine credibility, and sometimes do not even try to do so. Even where it is one word against another and differing witness accounts cannot resolve the matter, you must still resolve credibility issues. Inexperienced investigators frequently place themselves into positions in which, even if they wanted to resolve credibility, they are not able to do so. Another problem occurs when investigators attempt to resolve credibility when the key witnesses have only been interviewed by telephone.

Making a Determination. Sometimes it is the word of one witness against another, and their stories are diametrically opposed. Some investigators simply conclude, as a result, that no determination can be made. There may be times when you cannot decide what you think happened. But this should be the exception and not the rule. You are expected to make a determination in your investigation. Do not avoid reaching a conclusion out of the fear of being wrong. Reach a reasonable conclusion as to the matters under investigation. It does not mean that it has to be the same amount of certainty that would apply in a criminal prosecution.

Offering Opinions. Do not opinions regarding the guilt or innocence of anyone involved. Observations are permissible, but the focus should be on whether the facts elicited during the investigation make your conclusions self-evident.

These errors may, in some jurisdictions, lead to claims for negligent investigation. Even if the claim cannot be made, the results of the investigation are compromised because of these mistakes.

> **Process Pointer:** By understanding the legal landmines, a conscientious investigator can step carefully in his pursuit of relevant information.

Poor Planning

The investigation must be well-planned and executed with a definite objective and strategy. The failure to plan each step of the investigation and consider the potential consequences of each step places the company at risk for serious problems including:

- Damage to the company's reputation.
- Damage to employee morale.
- Creation of evidence that can be used in future criminal or civil cases.
- Possible full-blown government investigation and sanctions.
- The investigation will provide no protection in private litigation.
- The investigation makes future misconduct possible.
- The investigation wastes corporate assets.

Obstruction of Justice

Responding to allegations of misconduct requires skill to avoid making a bad situation worse. Obstruction of justice arises when the government is involved, and the government's inquiries were somehow impeded or hindered. If improper of careless methods are used in a workplace investigation, it can appear later on as if the company was trying to cover up violations or distort a witness' testimony.

Compounding a Felony

The right to punish or to forgive a criminal is reserved to the state and federal governments. Individual and corporate victims do not have the right to do that. Agreeing to accept something of value in return for nor prosecuting—or for not reporting the crime to prosecutors—is itself a crime. It can result in legal punishment for the investigator and the company.

> **Process Pointer:** In some states, the promise not to report the matter to the police in exchange for something of value—money or information—is also considered extortion. It is a crime. Never promise the implicated person that you will or will not contact the police. Make your decision independent of him.

Whistleblower Protection

There are a variety of federal and state laws to protect whistleblowers. If an investigation shows that someone who is a whistleblower is also someone who completely fabricated a claim to harass another person, the company should still weigh the effects and application of any whistleblower statute that may apply. A possible situation may involve a person who has properly engaged in some improper conduct and fears that it is about to be discovered. He may file a whistleblower claim with authorities to cloak themselves in the whistleblower protections.

Retaliation

Those who are the source of a report and those who cooperate in an investigation are legally protected from retaliation. Ensure that the company does not take any unwarranted action against the employee that might appear to be retaliation for filing a report or cooperating with an investigation. Regardless of the legal implications of retaliation, the practical effect is that employees will only provide information in an investigation if they believe that they will not be penalized for doing so. You should therefore remain alert to any signs of retaliation.

Retaliation may take a variety of forms:

- A negative performance evaluation.
- A failure to receive a promotion.
- Receiving lower quality work assignments.
- Being excluded from meetings and decision making.
- A reduced level of salary increase, bonus or other pay treatment.
- Being taunted or ostracized by colleagues or a manager.
- The person or their property being subjected to harm.

You should be sufficiently conscious to the risk of retaliation and how to deal with it:

- Investigators should anticipate who may be the target of possible retaliation.
- Remind the relevant managers of individuals who may be the target of retaliatory behavior to be aware of the risk and of their obligation to prevent and/or stop retaliation of any kind.
- Remind each person interviewed that any person who, in good faith, seeks advice, raises a concern, reports misconduct or cooperates in an investigation is following the company's code of conduct and doing the right thing.
- Make sure each witness understands the company's non-retaliation policy, and that it is enforced vigorously.
- If an individual alleges that he has been the victim of retaliation, the Investigations Manager should be contacted immediately.

Discrimination

The investigations process must be consistently applied. This can be a particular problem when the process is first implemented, and where discipline is imposed in situations where it had not been before. Differences in treatment of employees invite allegations of discrimination of one form or another. There is also the risk that the sanctions applied later on to particular types of violations could have a disparate impact on the workforce and add to the appearance of discrimination.

When investigating claims of discrimination in the workplace, investigators must avoid the risk of discriminating themselves. For example, a worker complaining of religious discrimination may, in turn, claim that the employer engaged in religious discrimination by willingly failing to conduct an inadequate investigation. Conversely, over-investigating could similarly lead to complaints of "profiling" certain employees as possible investigation targets.

> **Process Pointer:** The failure to conduct a reasonable investigation risks a lawsuit by the implicated person—or even an implicated person in another similar investigation—for a variety of legal claims.

Invasion of Privacy

During investigative interviews, especially those involving sexual harassment, investigators may have to explore sensitive areas of personal conduct. You must recognize your employees' reasonable expectations of privacy. Questioning employees concerning activities that are not sufficiently related to their job performance conduct at work or relations with the subject of the investigation may constitute an invasion of privacy. Violating the right of privacy exposes the company to liability. The key here is to be cautious.

This claim generally has three elements: (i) an intentional intrusion, (ii) upon the claimant's private affairs or concerns, and (iii) that a reasonable person would find offensive. A well-recognized defense to an invasion-of-privacy claim is consent. However, the truth of the information is not the same thing as consent. Companies should draft appropriate policies and

Unless handled appropriately, the company may face serious legal exposure.

procedures to minimize privacy expectations. Initiate investigations only on the basis of documented factual allegations which objectively justify the investigation. Narrow the scope of any investigation to what is reasonable and necessary to protect the company's business interests. Finally, the information should be kept confidential and shared only with those who need to know it. Remember that your company has a legitimate right to conduct investigations in the workplace.

Defamation

Investigators must be sensitive to claims of defamation. This is a commonly alleged claim in workplace investigations. Investigators must be careful not to draw unwarranted conclusions or make unfounded accusations against investigation subjects. Defamatory communication is communication which, among other things, injures that person's reputation as to diminish respect, goodwill or confidence in which that person is held. Defamation may arise in the context of compliance communications. Communicating those conclusions and accusations to third parties constitutes "publication" of that information for defamation purposes. This can include warning statements, investigative reports, performance evaluations and statements in management meetings.

To minimize this risk, investigators should explicitly detail the factual basis for any conclusions about individual culpability. Cautionary language should be used where possible. Supporting facts should be verified. The conclusions drawn should be reasonably justified by the facts. Do not use caustic, hyperbolic or otherwise colorful language. The report should also be distributed on a limited basis to avoid a claim of excessive publication.

Truth is a defense to a defamation claim. A qualified privilege may also exist where the statement was believed by the employer in good faith when it was made, the statement served a legitimate purpose, the statement was limited in scope, and was "published" to an individual who also had a legitimate business interest in receiving the communication. Additionally, the company must not have reason to believe that the statements or questions are false and must not be acting with reckless disregard for the truth. But the company must also not exceed the scope of that privilege. Careful investigating, especially the reporting or discussion of investigation findings, reduces the risk to the company.

Libel

Many of the same considerations regarding defamation also apply to a possible libel claim. Useful investigation reports are both meticulous and frank. Questionable activities must be described in detail. In some investigations, the factual descriptions will be the equivalent of accusing someone of a crime or at least dishonesty.

False Imprisonment

An employee establishes a claim for false imprisonment when the employee establishes that he was confined unreasonably during the investigation. The risk of such a claim during an investigation is greatest when the subject is being interviewed. You have the right to question employees regarding conduct connected at work, and your company may require cooperation as a condition of employment. However, you may not detain an employee against his or her will, either physically or through threats. Unlawful detention can be accomplished by violence, threats or any means that restrain a person from moving from one place to another. You must be careful never to give the impression that the employee will be physically confined or restrained during the interview. You must always advise a witness that they have a clear option to leave the interview at any time. You should never attempt to prevent a witness from leaving the room or try to restrain the witness with threats. If the witness can show that the threat caused just fear of injury to their person, reputation or property, the company may be liable for damages.

Emotional Distress

An employee may claim emotional distress if an aggressive investigator conducts an interview in such a way that the employee feels unusually humiliated or threatened. These claims can be successful if the action is seen as offensive to a reasonable person and would be viewed as outrageous by a reasonable society. There is generally no valid reason for an investigator or anyone else to shout at a witness, use slurs or other demeaning language, or humiliate the employee.

Malicious Prosecution

Employers may be sued for malicious prosecution if they are not careful regarding the criminal prosecution of an employee. If an employee is reported to the police and described as some sort of criminal, but for some reason there turns out to be no basis for criminal charges, that employee may sue the employer for malicious prosecution. If an employee is suspected of wrongdoing, and under the circumstances it would be appropriate to get law enforcement involved, the better approach is to report to the law enforcement authorities whatever the problem is and make the information available. If the information happens to include the names of employees who may have material knowledge of a crime, the company should be able to defend against such a claim. It is not malicious prosecution to simply give factual information to the police and request their assistance.

Wrongful Discharge
If the investigation is not done properly, someone dismissed based on information discovered in the investigation may subsequently file a claim of wrongful discharge. A similar result may occur if the investigation is not conducted according to your established procedures. And while a company may decide to fire an employee based on the results of an investigation, there is no guarantee that a jury, looking at the findings with the benefit of hindsight, will agree with the company's conclusions.

C. Protecting the Findings from Disclosure

You must understand the applicable legal privileges and take affirmative action to ensure they apply to the fullest extent possible. Every effort must be taken and due diligence exercised to maintain the privileged nature of the investigation.

However, the purposes of the investigation process also include business improvement. There will also be pressures by executive management to see the fruits of the investigation. The desire to protect privileges should not override the fundamental need to use the organizational intelligence derived from the investigation process to improve the company's operations. Both the privileges and the investigation are meant to benefit the company. Moreover, the legal protection offered to investigative reports by these privileges is neither complete nor entirely predictable.

This requires a basic awareness—especially for non-lawyers—of what the privileges are, and what they do not cover. There is no ironclad method for preventing disclosure of investigative reports. Considering the broader dissemination of investigative information within companies, you should assume that any part of their investigations may be subject to production in a later proceeding.

The documents and other communications created during an investigation typically will not be privileged from disclosure to government regulators, private litigants or other third parties in litigation or other legal proceedings where the investigation may be relevant. This is often true even when a company attorney is involved. Accordingly, you should not rely on the privilege when generating documents. If there is any question about whether communications during an investigation can be protected from disclosure, the compliance officer should consult the company's legal department to determine whether privilege can or should apply and what steps are required in that particular situation to maintain it.

Privileges can be waived if the company discloses the privileged communication (intentionally or accidentally) to a third party or, in some cases, even to people within the company who are not within the scope of the privileged communication. Once the privilege over a particular communication has been waived, it cannot be reclaimed.

The investigation plan should set out whether the investigation is to be carried out on a privileged basis or not. Everyone involved in the investigation should know that no decision should be made to waive privileges applicable to a workplace investigation until after its conclusion. If a company decides before or during an investigation to waive an applicable privilege, it can be argued that subsequent communications are not privileged because they were not intended to be confidential. This can harm the company especially if the decision is made before potentially damaging facts are discovered in the investigation.

This section is intended only to give a brief overview of these important topics. Please consult your company's legal department for specific guidance when the preservation of these privileges is essential to the investigation strategy.

Confidentiality

The importance of keeping confidential all that relates to an investigation cannot be overemphasized. Maintaining confidentiality is critical to the integrity of an investigation. Failing to ensure strict confidentiality throughout all phases of an investigation may have serious consequences:

- Someone's reputation may be damaged if others learn of the allegation, regardless of whether the allegation is found to be true.
- The success of the investigation can be undermined if others know of the investigation.

- The implicated person might engage in cover-up activities when they learn that they are being investigated.
- The company might be vulnerable to negative publicity or liability.
- The company's ability to defend any legal action associated with the matter may be damaged.
- The disclosure of information (or misinformation) may cause retaliation.

Although the need for confidentiality begins when the report is received, it does not end with the conclusion of the investigation. The fact that an investigation is underway or is being considered, the subject matter of it, the process followed, the materials or information gathered and the results of the investigation must always be treated confidentially. These includes being careful before using the details of an investigation at some later point in time.

The Attorney-Client Privilege

It is well-settled than a company may invoke the attorney-client privilege. The privilege belongs solely to the corporation, not to any employee. There are several factors relevant to the availability of the attorney-client privilege in the context of a workplace investigation:

1. The communications were made by company employees under instructions from superiors in order for the company to secure legal advice from counsel;
2. The information needed by company counsel in order to formulate legal advice was not otherwise available to executive management;
3. The information communicated concerned matters within the scope of the employee's corporate duties;
4. The employees were aware that the reason for the communication with counsel was to enable the company to obtain legal advice; and
5. The communications were ordered to be kept confidential and they remain confidential.

The attorney-client privilege only protects the communication from discovery; the underlying information contained in the communication is discoverable. The privilege does not extent to the underlying facts.

Communications that merely transmit facts may be discoverable, because the privilege most often applies to requests for legal advice. The transfer of non-privileged documents from the corporation to the attorney similarly does not make the documents privileged. Communications made for purposes other than to obtain counsel's professional legal advice, including communications made to third parties are not privileged. Accordingly, simply funneling communications through a lawyer will not shield an investigation from disclosure because communications for business purposes are not privileged.

There are some best practices you should follow when your company believes it is essential to maintain the attorney-client privilege in a particular investigation:

- The investigation should be conducted by an attorney, preferably one who has had investigatory experience.
- If outside counsel is retained, the attorney-client relation should be established expressly at the outset of any agreement between the company and outside counsel. The agreement should state plainly that the outside attorney has been engaged solely to conduct the investigation and give advice to the board of directors.
- The attorney should state explicitly to all persons who are interviewed that he is serving as the company's attorney for the purpose of providing legal advice to the company.
- Documents should be kept under control. They should be marked "privileged and confidential" and maintained by counsel only.
- The temptation to use the workplace investigation as a defense in other litigation should be avoided, as this will waive the privilege.
- The company's employees should be instructed not to discuss the investigation or make public statements about it. Disclosures of privileged information should be limited to those with a need to know, narrowly defined, and do not reproduce privileged materials without authorization.
- When preparing written reports, keep them brief, general and evaluative.
- Ensure that interviews are summarized and include personal opinions in order to maximize the likelihood that the privilege will attach.
- Discard all unnecessary documentation generated during the investigation.

If an in-house counsel conducts the investigation, there are risks of waiving the attorney-client privilege. If the in-house counsel plays both a legal and a business role, then the in-house counsel should make a good-faith effort to make sure that all conversations and documents have a legal or a business purpose, but not a combination of both. Whether the conversation or document is legal or business should be expressly stated and documented.

If the company is concerned with an inadvertent waiver, any documentation upon which the company may need to rely on in litigation should be prepared by someone other than an inside attorney. This would include, for example, the company's ultimate findings and the basis for the findings. Similarly, the ultimate decision as to what did or did not happen should not be made by the attorney but by executive management. Finally, the attorney who represents the company in any court matter should be someone other than the attorney who participated in the investigation. If the facts disclosed in the investigation formed a basis for any employment decision, the lawyer becomes a potential witness.

The application of the attorney-client privilege to an in-house attorney conducting an investigation is questionable. First, the lawyer's task as an investigator requires compiling relevant facts to form a legal opinion. This blurs the distinction between investigative and legal activities. Second, as a participant in the corporation, the distinction blurs between the lawyer's role as business advisor and the role as a legal advisor. While it is true that the suspected violation of a legal violation triggers the investigation, that may not be sufficient to cloak the investigation under the attorney-client privilege.

The Work Product Doctrine

An attorney's work-product, including factual investigation in the course of an investigation, is subject to qualified protection. The objective of the privilege is to protect an attorney's trial preparation from exploitation by an adverse party of prepared in anticipation of litigation. However, in contrast to the attorney-client privilege, the work-product privilege is not absolute. An adverse party can obtain discovery of the documents if that party makes a proper application to the court.

Work product includes (i) material prepared or mental impressions developed in anticipation of litigation by or for a party or a party's representatives; and (ii) communications made in anticipation of litigation or for trial between a party and the party's representatives, or among the parties representatives. The doctrine protects the attorney's thought process and issue formulation. The doctrine also protects the mechanical compilation of information to the extent the compilation reveals the attorney's thought processes.

The work-product privilege is broader than the attorney-client privilege because the work-product privilege protects communications with non-attorneys. But the work-product privilege is narrower in that the communication must be in anticipation of litigation or in preparation for trial.

For the work-product privilege to apply, litigation need not be imminent, but the documents must have been prepared because of the prospect of litigation. However, documents prepared in the ordinary course of business fall outside the scope of the work-product privilege, even if litigation is imminent.

The work-product privilege distinguishes between "fact" work product and "opinion" work product. The former means work product that reflects certain facts, rather than mental impressions. This type of work product can be discovered when a judge decides there is a substantial need and to avoid undue hardship. Lawyers conducting investigations should ensure that their mental impressions are included wherever possible in all written materials.

Opinion work product is generally regarded as non-discoverable. Therefore, attorneys taking notes during employee interviews should intersperse those notes with evaluations of the witness' candor and the attorney's legal theories appropriate to the facts observed. Adverse parties may not obtain documents that contact the mental impressions, conclusions, opinions or legal theories of any attorney concerning litigation. Also, while factual data is not ordinarily protected from discovery, where documents are assembled by or at a lawyer's direction in anticipation of litigation, discovery is precluded to prevent revealing the lawyer's thought processes.

The Self-Evaluative Privilege

The attorney-client privilege and work-product privilege do not protect materials that are not communications for the purpose of obtaining legal advice or that are not prepared in anticipation of litigation. Reports and other documents that may be intended to be confidential are frequently discoverable in litigation.

In some court jurisdictions, however, there is a recognized privilege for self-critical analysis on public policy grounds. The rationale behind this privilege is consistent with that favoring protection of workplace investigative reports from disclosure. Those jurisdictions apparently wish to encourage companies and other entities to internally examine their operations and to improve them. Documents protected under this privilege have satisfied each of these criteria: (i) the report was the result of a critical self-analysis by the party seeking the protection; (ii) the public has a strong interest in maintaining the free flow of information of the kind sought; and (iii) the information is of the type whose flow would be stifled without protection. To these requirements should be added the general proviso that no document will be privileged unless it was prepared with the expectation that it would be kept confidential, and that it has in fact been kept confidential.

The majority of federal courts have refused to recognize the privilege when presented in any context, especially when the information sought is factual rather than analytical or evaluative information. Ultimately, the decision as to the level of documentation carried out during the investigation process is one for each company to make independently, based on the company's own circumstances.

> **Process Pointer:** For all intents, the legal privileges are worthless to protect the investigation documents—including final reports and memos—from disclosure in a lawsuit or prosecution. Additionally, the facts stated in investigation documents come from other sources, such as witnesses and documents that could be obtained directly from those sources. Instead, make the investigation documents professional and objectively complete. Never write anything on paper that you would not be comfortable explaining in a courtroom.

D. Referrals to Law Enforcement

In the current business environment, companies usually turn to their compliance staff to investigate allegations of employee misconduct. The broad scope of internal codes of conduct and Sarbanes-Oxley obligations means that investigations today occur more often, cover a wider spectrum of circumstances, and likely detect more misconduct than in the past. Combine this with increased opportunities for criminal behavior due to increasingly complex business structures, dispersed operations, and technology advances, and the opportunities for crime by insiders are not likely to lessen in the future. The costs to companies of internal misconduct are significant: it is estimated that the typical business loses five percent of its revenue annually to workplace fraud alone.

Some of your investigations will conclude that the company was the victim of a crime. Your findings will present management with three options: reporting the matter to the police—local, state, or federal law enforcement authorities—for possible prosecution, filing a civil lawsuit, and/or pursuing claims against third parties and their insurers.

If your company is typical, when some crime is suspected, they want the police to swoop down, make some arrests, and cart the bad guys off to jail. However, if executive management wants to report the matter to the police for possible criminal action against the wrongdoers, they must be counseled carefully. The company must consider the benefits and risks of some important points.

Business Goals

The referral of the matter to the police should never be simply a knee-jerk reaction. The referral must further a business purpose. You must, therefore, identify the company's goal in referring the matter to the police. Does the company simply want the satisfaction of having reported it to the police, regardless of what happens after the report is made? (This can be useful if the company wants to publicize it internally as a deterrent to others.) Would simply the arrest of the wrongdoer be sufficient, regardless of whether he is convicted? Does the company want the wrongdoers punished or to send a public message to its marketplace? The company must make this decision at the outset because it affects the internal preparation of the referral and the amount of resources the company should expect to devote later on to achieve its desired result.

The Company's Reputation

Although executive management may feel that they are vindicating the company's rights by contacting the police, it is nonetheless a public act. If the wrongdoing was enabled by some internal business failure, the company will be announcing that failure to its customers and competitors. The company may also be saying, although indirectly, that it has hired dishonest people. This may lead to questions by shareholders and the marketplace about the competence of management.

On the other hand, your company may view the referral as an act of institutional hygiene, and that it shows that the company is committed to the highest ethical standards. (It may also highlight the efficacy of your company's compliance program.) The referral shows that compliance-minded senior managers "walk the talk." The important point is to consider fully the varying perceptions the referral will have.

Contacting an Agency

Now that executive management has decided to report the matter to the police, which agency do you contact? Naturally, you want the best agency to handle your case. Remember, however, that your choice may be among a number of law enforcement agencies with jurisdiction. Federal criminal laws cover most of the common misconduct committed by company employees, including various types of fraud, interstate transport of stolen property, commercial bribery, intellectual property crimes, and racketeering. State criminal laws cover most of the same conduct. Therefore, a criminal act that can be prosecuted by federal authorities may also be prosecuted by state or local ones.

Take the time to choose the right one in light of the nature of the crime, its complexity, the dollar amounts involved, and the location of the incident. Although your executive management may feel comforted to know that a high-profile agency like the FBI or Secret Service has the case, a referral to local or state police, while less glamorous, might produce a faster and more meaningful result for your company.

However, do not shop your case around to a number of agencies. One of the first questions you will be asked when the report is taken is whether any other agency has been contacted. Whether for reasons of resources or turf, many agencies do not take a case that another agency is handling, even if that other agency only took some nominal steps. This is also why the decision to contact the police and the initial contact must be coordinated by executive management. A well-intentioned manager who called the police to make a report when he first suspected wrongdoing may prevent you from having any other agency—especially a more appropriate agency—take the case.

Timing

Time your initial contact properly. Do not contact the police prematurely. The police cannot investigate every allegation, so wait until you have developed sufficient facts to explain—and document—what happened.

Remember, of course, that the investigation will only be one matter that competes for the resources of the police. Their world is a fluid one, and it is full of unexpected shifts in resources. Business-related investigations often give way to more urgent police matters. Police detectives and government agents are very busy, with many matters under investigation and prosecution. Unless the magnitude of the misconduct is such that it is deemed a priority, the investigation will proceed as resources allow, and that may mean waiting for an extended period of time.

Sympathy

You must make your company appear sympathetic. Police and prosecutors deal on a daily basis with violent crimes and other inhumanity. Those victims motivate the authorities. The authorities, in contrast, may view the crime you report as the result of poor business practices that created the opportunity for the problem rather than seeing the company as someone's victim. This is where the importance of emphasizing your compliance program comes in. An effective program shows that the company takes proactive measures to ensure that the company and its employees act ethically, and that the company has affirmatively prohibited the conduct in question. your company may then be perceived as having been victimized despite its own efforts to protect itself.

Case Complexity

When you get the opportunity to present what your workplace investigation found, don't let your case appear too complex. You must be able to summarize the case in one sentence. Otherwise, there is little realistic hope that it will be meaningfully investigated.

The police deal with serious crimes on a daily basis. It is relatively easy for them to assemble the evidence to prove, for example, the elements of a robbery. This is their world. The corporate world, with its policies, compliance processes, hierarchies and business units, is not that familiar to them.

Don't expect the police to embrace the complexity of your business operations as a chance for them to expand their knowledge. Most lack a business background, and they may not readily confess to you that they do not understand the machinations of how you do business. Consequently, authorities may focus on what is familiar to them and ignore your report.

You must be prepared to overcome their reluctance. One way to do this is by "gift-wrapping" the investigation. Marshal the known facts into an objective report. Organize copies of key documents. Document the chain of custody for them. Build a paper-trail or chronology of what you believe happened. Provide a list of witnesses. Offer an expert witness from your company, if necessary. Prepare charts, graphs, maps or other demonstrative aids. Be prepared to break down the incident into simple terms that a layman could follow. Also, be prepared to identify potential problems or factual gaps. The more complete and documented your package of information, the more likely it is to be prosecuted.

Present the case to the police personally, not over the telephone. This will demonstrate your company's commitment to the process.

Cooperation

Be prepared to cooperate fully. Although you may not always have the opportunity, depending on the agency, you should try to expand your role from that of a victim to being part of the investigative team.

Assign a single point of contact to facilitate all company-related inquiries and to ensure quick access to people, documents and information. Offer to be a company translator, guide and intermediary for the police. Get senior managers involved to show their commitment. Most importantly, remember that the police and prosecutors will approach the case in terms of probable cause and burdens of proof. Everything you do that helps them to address those factors lessens the chances that your case will not be prosecuted.

However, be prepared to surrender all control over the investigation after the referral. Police and prosecutors control their investigations. They may also insist that the company take no further action on its own to avoid compromising a possible criminal prosecution.

For some significant investigations, you should also recognize that the criminal investigation may interfere with the company's ability to carry on business. The police may need access to computer systems, personnel, and business records. Your investigation, however comprehensive, does not prevent the police from making their own inquiries, and they likely will anyway.

Prosecutor Resources

If the investigation is fruitful, the evidence will then be reported to the prosecutor. This is a crucial step in the process. Any police agency will take a report of possible criminal activity. Your goal is the prosecution of the wrongdoers.

You must focus on what it takes to capture the prosecutor's interest in prosecuting the wrongdoers. This may not be easy. For example, due to demands of police, prosecutors fail to pursue 75 percent of bank check fraud cases. According to the U.S. Government Accountability Office, in large cities where a majority of resources are used to prosecute violent crime, the percentage rises to 90 percent.

With limited resources, the prosecutor has broad discretion to decide not to prosecute, even if the company and the police believe the case is a compelling one. You should acknowledge this reality and help build a case that (i) would be attractive to a jury, (ii) present the company as a sympathetic victim, and (iii) has sufficient proof to justify a verdict beyond a reasonable doubt. Don't be afraid to use some salesmanship. If your case has some hook to catch the prosecutor's interest—dollar amount, organized-crime involvement, headline-grabbing facts—be sure to emphasize it.

You must remember that the government has different objectives than your company. They are focused on righting the wrongs against society, not the wrong done to your company. Your company's goal could be sidelined by plea bargains, cooperating testimony, and political factors. External factors, such as national-security demands on federal agencies, may also affect the results your company seeks. Finally, the prosecutor may make decisions about charging, settlement or strategy with which the company may not agree.

Be Realistic

You must be prepared to temper management expectations. Managers must be educated on the realistic outcome of the referral. Their likely vision of someone being led out in handcuffs—known as the "perp walk"—will rarely occur. The time needed for these prosecutions will not usually be as quick as management would like. Minor offenses may not be severely punished, and jail time may not be likely. Senior managers must understand that a referral may neither bring a prompt resolution of the matter nor will it necessarily bring prompt restitution. There is just no "magic bullet" to help a company that is victimized by crime.

In most cases, contacting the police should be used as a last resort when other options will not work. And it should never be considered as just another step in your company's incident-management process. The best approach is to solve your business problem first. The police can be contacted if the company then wants to prosecute. And if executive management fully supports the referral and appreciates its benefits and risks, your efforts may be worth it.

Criminal Recovery and Restitution

The criminal courts provide for victim restitution, and this is frequently ordered as an attempt to make the victim whole. In reality, this is ineffective for your company. Few defendants every pay any of the restitution they have been ordered to pay.

Do not look to the criminal courts to recover from those who steal or commit fraud against your company. You are asking for disappointment. Do not allow your company's leadership to make the criminal court system part of your recovery strategy.

> **Process Pointer:** When you involve law enforcement in any investigation, you decrease your chances of success and double the cost of the investigation. Because the company now loses control of the decision-making, the investigation will be drawn out to meet the needs of the police and the prosecutor.

CONCLUSION

The success of your workplace investigations process depends on your vision for the unit. That vision will allow the process to progress and meet the increasing challenges that your company faces. Hardly anyone inherits an investigations process in good shape. The first challenge is how to achieve an organizational presence.

This book has presented the reader with a variety of bullet-point lists of things to consider. In conclusion, one more list should be offered—the things you should consider when formulating the vision:

- Give significant thought to where your company is right now in its investigation of workplace misconduct.
- Decide what is important to your company when investigating misconduct.
- Determine where you want the workplace investigations unit to be in the future.
- Visualize what that target goal would look like.
- Condense the vision into a specific strategic plan.
- Link that plan to performance objectives and measures.
- Develop a way to educate business executives and investigators regarding the goals.
- Determine how you will secure the resources necessary to achieve these goals.

One of the most effective risk-management tools available to a company is a properly conducted investigation. The best way to conduct investigations depends on a number of considerations, as this book has tried to explain. Workplace investigations require the application of specialized skills and knowledge, and these cannot be developed ad hoc when the needs for an investigation arise. Companies must develop their workplace investigation function proactively and as a business function. Taking these actions will improve your company's ability to investigate misconduct, remedy any problems, improve processes, and minimize your company's liability in any related lawsuits.

SOURCES

Assoc. of Certified Fraud Examiners, *2006 Fraud Examiners Manual* (2006).

Assoc. of Certified Fraud Examiners, *2006 Report to the Nation on Occupational Fraud and Abuse* (2006).

Babitsky, Steven and James J. Mangraviti, *Writing and Defending your Expert Report* (Seak 2002).

Bologna, Jack and Paul Shaw, *Corporate Crime Investigation* (Butterworth-Heinemann 1997).

Booden, Michael R., *Conducting Effective Internal Investigations* (2004), at *http://www.acca.com*.

Bratton, Eleanor and Daniel Long, *Compliance Investigations: Avoiding Common Mistakes* (1995), at *http://www.modrall.com*.

Brennan, James and Jeffrey Kaplan, "Making Compliance Training Effective," *GC New York* (July 25, 2005).

Brian, Brad and Barry McNeil, *Compliance Corporate Investigations* (American Bar Association 2003).

Cole, Richard, *Management of Compliance Business Investigations: A Survival Guide* (Charles Thomas 1996).

Conducting Compliance Investigations (Association of Certified Fraud Examiners 2003) at *http://www.acfe.com*.

Corporate Compliance (October 2004) at *http://www.acca.com/resource/v4955*.

Council Toolkit: Conducting Internal Investigations, Compliance and Ethics Leadership Council (2004), at *http://www.celc.executiveboard.com/CELC/1,3229,0-0-Protected_Display-131447-14160*.

Dempsey, John S., *Introduction to Investigations* (Thomson Wadsworth 2003).

Duggan, Sarah Helene, *Compliance Corporate Investigations: Legal Ethics, Professionalism and the Employee Interview*, 2003 Colum. Bus. L. Rev 859 (2003).

Edwards, Deborah L., Mark Colloway and Brian Edwards, *What to Do When the Whistle Blows: Do's and Don'ts of Compliance Investigations* (2004) at *http://www.acca.com*.

Employing Legal Privilege to Protect Compliance Audits and Risk Assessments, Corporate Senior Manager Board (2005), at *http://www.generalcounselroundtable.com*.

Ferraro, Eugene F., *Investigations in the Workplace* (Auerbach Publications 2006).

Frank, Jonny J., *The Role of the Forensic Accountant in Internal Corporate Investigations* (2003), at *http://www.som.yale.edu/faculty/Sunder/FinancialFraud.doc*.

Haig, Robert, *Successful Partnering between Inside and Outside Counsel* (Thomson West 2004).

Hancock, William (ed.), *Corporate Counsel's Guide to Legal Audits and Investigations* (Business Laws, Inc. 2005).

Harrison, Orrin, *Conducting Corporate Investigations under the Increased Scrutiny of Sarbanes-Oxley* (2003), at *http://www.akingump.com/docs/publication/678.pdf*.

Hasl-Kelchner, Hanna, *The Business Guide to Legal Literacy* (Jossey-Bass 2006).

Hogge, Raymond L., "How to Conduct a Lawful Workplace Investigation," Virginia Labor Law (June 1998), at *http://www.virginialaborlaw.com/library/adr/article-investigation.htm*.

Investigations Management (ASIS 2006).

Johnson, William C., *Liar, Liar, Pants on Fire: How to Establish an Effective Compliance Investigations Program* (2002), at *http://www.acca.com*.

Kahn Consulting, Inc., *How to Conduct a Corporate Internal Investigations Reference Materials* (2004), at *http://www.acca.com/protected/article/internali/kahn.html*.

Koletar, Joseph W., *Fraud Exposed* (John Wiley & Sons 2003).

Kuehne, Benedict, *Protecting the Privilege in the Corporate Setting: Conducting and Defending Compliance Corporate Investigations*, 9 St. Thomas L. Rev. 651 (1997).

MacKillop, Malcolm, *The Reason Harassment Probes Fail* (2004), at *http://www.workopolis.com*.

Managing the Risk of Fraud: A Guide for Managers (May 2003), at *http://www.hm-treasury.gov.uk*.

Marmer, Ronald L., *How to Conduct Internal Corporate Investigations after Sarbanes-Oxley* (2005), at *http://www.Jenner.com/efiles*.

Martin, Jay, *Conducting an Effective Compliance Corporate Investigation* (2002), at *http://www.winstead.com/articles*.

McMahon, Rory J., *Practical Handbook for Professional Investigators* (CRC Press 2007).

Michael, William and Mark Larsen, *Compliance Investigations* (2004), at *http://www.acca.com/inforpaks/intinvest.html*.

Muller, Deborah, "As the Table Turns: How to Maintain the Upper Hand When Conducting a Workplace Investigation," *Workforce Management Online* (November 2007), at *http://www.workforce.com/section/03/features*.

Pfadenhauer, Diane M., Workplace Investigations: Rethinking the Traditional Paradigm and Advocating the Use of Third-Party Investigators, HR Advisor (July 2005), at *http://www.thehrlawyer.com*.

Poteet, Dewey, *How to Conduct an Effective Workplace Investigation* (2001), at *http://www.akingump.com*

Propper, Eugene, *Corporate Fraud Investigations and Compliance Programs* (Oceana Publications 2000).

Rabon, Don, *Interviewing and Interrogation* (Carolina Academic Press 1992).

Rabon, Don, *Investigative Discourse Analysis* (Carolina Academic Press 2003).

Richards, Dave, "Envisioning our Future," *Internal Auditor* (August 2001).

Safeguarding the Corporation, Corporate Senior Manager Board (2006), at *http://www.celc.senior managerboard.com/ DocId=96893*.

Schiff, Matthew B. and Linda C. Kramer, "Conducting Internal Investigations of Employee Theft and Other Misconduct," *The Brief* (Spring 2004) at *http://www.aba.org*.

Sennewald, Charles A. and John Tsukayama, *The Process of Investigation: Concepts and Strategies for Investigators in the Private Sector* (Elsevier 2006).

Shenk, Maury D. and Melanie Schneck, "Should a Corporation Report a Breach to Law Enforcement," *Secure Business Quarterly* (3rd Qtr. 2001).

Silverstein, Ira, *Hear No Evil, See No Evil No Longer Viable*, Outside Counsel (2005), at *http://www.acca.com*.

Steinberg, Marc I., *Attorney Liability after Sarbanes-Oxley* (Law Journal Press 2005).

Taylor, David F., "What if It's an Inside Job," *Business Law Today* (September/October 2005).

The CPA's Handbook of Fraud and Commercial Crime Prevention (American Institute of Certified Public Accountants 2003).

T*he Ethical Minefield for In-House Counsel* (2003), at *http://www.acca.com/protected/article/internali/minefield.html*.

Thompson, John, "How to Conduct an Effective Investigation," *CIO* (June 6, 2007) at *http://www.cio.com/article/print/117452*.

Turner, Jonathan, "Steps to Take When Referring your Case for Prosecution," *Preventing Business Fraud* (March 2002).

Webb, Dan K., *Corporate Compliance Investigations* (Law Journal Press 2004).

Welch, Jack, *Winning* (Harper Business 2005).

Wells, Joseph, "Let Them Know Someone's Watching," *Journal of Accountancy*, (May 2002), at *http://www.aicpa.org*.

Wells, Joseph, "New Approaches to Fraud Deterrence," *Journal of Accountancy*, (Feb. 2004), at *http://www.aicpa.org*.

Wells, Joseph, "Why Employees Commit Fraud," *Journal of Accountancy*, (Feb. 2001), at *http://www.aicpa.org*.

Yeschke, Charles, *The Art of Investigative Interviewing* (Butterworth Heinemann 2003).

APPENDIX A

Compliance & Ethics Issue Reporting and Response Policy

1 Applicability and Responsibility
   (a) This Policy applies to all employees of the Company and replaces all previous policies concerning this subject.
   (b) Each employee and agent is responsible for ensuring that his or her actions comply with this Policy. Each manager is responsible for his or her department's compliance and for informing his or her employees and agents about this Policy.

2 Basis and Object
   (a) This Policy specifies the manner in which the Company shall report, receive, retain and respond to compliance and ethics issues, including, but not limited to, the Company's accounting, accounting controls and auditing matters, that are reported by colleagues, associates or others. This Policy also strictly prohibits discharging, harassing, discriminating or taking any adverse action against any employee or agent in the terms and conditions of employment because of any lawful act done to provide information to assist in a Company or government investigation or proceeding involving an alleged violation of law or company policy.
   (b) This Policy is mandatory for all employees.
   (c) The purpose of this Policy is to comply with all applicable legal requirements regarding the reporting, receipt, retention, and response to compliance and ethics issues including, without limitation, those matters arising under the "Code of Conduct" in the Company. The focus shall be on business and professional standards of conduct, compliance with applicable law, good

corporate citizenship, prevention and detection of misconduct, and the identification of areas of particular risk to the Company.

(d) The purpose of this Policy is also to facilitate the measurement and reporting of reported incidents of possible compliance or ethics-related misconduct on a Company-wide basis to the Corporate Governance Committee and the Audit Committee of the Board of Directors.

3 Definitions and Explanations

(a) By using the term "Misconduct," we mean any fraud or violation of law, company policy, procedure or ethical standard of conduct by the Company or any of its employees or agents. Misconduct includes each of the categories of personal conduct described in the appendix to this Policy.

(b) By using the term "Company," we mean all legal entities/business units which are part of _____ and their respective employees and agents.

(c) By using the term "Ethics Office," we mean the Company's Corporate Compliance Department.

(d) By using the term "Company officer," we mean any CEO, CFO, COO, General Counsel, and other such senior manager officers, senior financial officers or other members of senior Company management.

(e) By using the term "Guide to Conducting an Investigation," we mean the guidance document issued by the Ethics Office setting forth the procedures to be followed in investigating allegations of Misconduct.

(f) By using the term "Company agents," we mean all non-employees of the company who are properly authorized to act on the Company's behalf.

(g) By using the term "Company Compliance & Ethics Line," we mean the reporting system Company has contracted with a third party to provide a mechanism to confidentially and anonymously report any observed or suspected instances of Misconduct. The Company Compliance & Ethics Line is available to call, toll free, 24 hours a day, seven days a week and can take calls in almost any language at the following telephone numbers:

United States & Canada:

Outside the United States & Canada: (Country Access Number)

The Company Compliance & Ethics Line can also be contacted on the Internet at www._____.com.

(h) By using the term "Report," we mean an incident of actual or suspected Misconduct that is reported to a manager, an appropriate department head, Internal Audit, the Legal Department, Human Resources Department, the Ethics Office, the Board of Directors or the Company Compliance & Ethics Line.

4 Procedures, Rules and Guidelines
(a) Responsibility for Reporting Misconduct:
- All Company employees and Company agents are obligated to report any observed instances of Misconduct to either their manager, an appropriate department head, Internal Audit, the Legal Department, Human Resources Department, the Ethics Office, the Board of Directors or the Company Compliance & Ethics Line.
- Once reported, the manager, department head, Internal Audit, the Legal Department, and/or Human Resources Department shall take all necessary steps to ensure that the Ethics Office has been informed of the Report, regardless of the manner in which the report shall be investigated. This is to allow the Ethics Office to track these reports centrally for the Company. The Ethics Office and other key internal departments shall establish a process by which the Ethics Office shall be effectively and expeditiously informed.
- The Ethics Office shall establish and administer a process by which other key internal departments shall be notified of the receipt by the Ethics Office of a Report. That department may, at its election, appropriately participate in the investigation.
- The Ethics Office shall ensure that the process by which Reports are taken, processed, investigated and reported complies with local law and regulation in the jurisdiction where a Report is made.

(b) Response to Reports of Misconduct
- The Ethics Office has primary responsibility to ensure that a detailed, competent and appropriate investigation of the Report has occurred.
- The Ethics Office shall either perform, or arrange for, a professional, independent and objective investigation. The resources devoted to such investigations should be proportionate to the nature of the Report. The Ethics Office should use the resources available in the Legal Department, Human Resources Department, or

Internal Audit as appropriate, to ensure the independence and objectivity of all investigations of Reports.
— The Ethics Office shall ensure that Company employees who investigate Reports are competent and adequately trained for that purpose. The Ethics Office shall provide or arrange for such training when needed. The Ethics Office shall also ensure that the investigation process is consistently applied throughout the Company.
— The purposes of an investigation of a Report shall include (i) to determine if the specific allegation(s) of Misconduct are substantiated by the facts elicited, (ii) whether other Misconduct may have occurred, (iii) to identify areas of potential risk (financial or legal) to the Company as a result of the Misconduct, and (iv) to identify areas of business operations which may require improvement as a result of the Misconduct. The Ethics Office shall have the discretion to determine the appropriate scope of an investigation.
— Once an investigation is completed and findings are made, the Ethics Office or investigator shall (i) provide appropriate feedback to the person or persons who made the Report regarding the outcome of the investigation; and (ii) advise the responsible management as to the specific facts determined by the investigation to allow management to take actions, as may be appropriate in the circumstances, to discipline any Company employees who engaged in Misconduct. The Ethics Office should also recommend any needed improvements in policies and procedures to avoid repetition of the Misconduct.
— The investigation shall be conducted according to the protocols specified in the Guide to Conducting an Investigation.
— All allegations of Misconduct regarding any Company officer who is not a member of the Ethics Office shall be immediately forwarded to the Ethics Office for investigation. The Ethics Office shall have responsibility for performing or overseeing any investigation regarding the alleged Misconduct of such Company officers to ensure independence and objectivity.
— All allegations of Misconduct by the members of the Ethics Office shall be immediately forwarded to the Corporate Governance Committee of the Board of Directors who shall

have responsibility for overseeing all investigations regarding the alleged Misconduct of the members of the Ethics Office to ensure independence and objectivity.
— All Reports received by the Ethics Office (and associated investigation findings) shall be recorded by the Ethics Office in its Report database. This information, whether on an aggregate or investigation-specific basis, shall be made appropriately available to other departments and the Company's auditors.
— The Ethics Office shall take all necessary steps to protect the confidentiality, sensitivity and applicable legal protections for this information from unnecessary disclosure. The identity of a Company employee or a Company agent who has made a Report shall be protected to the extent possible, consistent with this Policy and applicable law.

(c) Periodic Summary Reports and Evaluation
— The Ethics Office shall summarize and periodically report to Company Executive management and the Corporate Governance and Audit Committee of the Board of Directors information regarding Reports and the Company's response thereto with regard to matters that are reported to the Ethics Office.
— The Ethics Office shall work with executive management to evaluate instances of Misconduct and determine whether changes to policies, procedures, training, monitoring, audits, control systems or other steps must be taken to prevent or reduce the possibility of such Misconduct occurring in the future.

(d) Contacting the Board of Directors
— Employees, investors or other interested parties may report instances of Misconduct directly to the Board of Directors by either calling one of the telephone numbers or writing to the address provided below:

_____
_____
_____
_____

If calling from outside of the United States or Canada, dial the AT&T Country Access Number, then, when prompted, dial (800)

(Note: Those calling from outside the United States or Canada can obtain their country AT&T Access Number by logging on to: *www.usa.att.com/traveler/index.jsp*.) Correspondence to the Board of Directors should be mailed to: Company Board of Directors Helpline

_____

_____

_____

— Calls and written correspondence made to the Board of Directors via the phone numbers or address provided above shall be received 24 hours a day, seven days a week by a third party service provider with whom Company has contracted to receive such messages on the Company's behalf. When the service provider receives either a telephone call or written correspondence directed to one or more of the Company's directors, the service provider shall fax correspondence and email call reports to Company's Chief Senior manager Officer, Chief Financial Officer, Chief Compliance Officer and General Counsel. These corporate officers shall then review the written correspondence and call reports to facilitate the delivery of such correspondence to the Company's Directors and to recommend, what if, any action should be taken in response to the correspondence or call reports.

— All call reports or correspondence shall be forwarded to the intended board member(s) unless they are of a trivial nature or otherwise not related to accounting, internal controls, auditing matters, corporate governance, safety, health or environmental issues or any other significant legal or ethical issues at Company. However, a report shall be made to the Corporate Governance Committee and Audit Committee of any correspondence not forwarded to the Board of Directors, and all such reports and correspondence shall be preserved and made available to any Directors who wish to review it.

5 Retaliation

Company employees and Company agents are strictly prohibited from discharging, harassing, discriminating or taking any adverse action against any employee in the terms and conditions of employment because of (i) any lawful act done to provide information to assist in a Company or government investigation or proceeding involving alleged Misconduct; or (ii) the employee made a Report honestly and in good faith. However, this provision does not protect a reporting Company employee from disciplinary action resulting from his or her own Misconduct.

6 Record Keeping

Records of all investigations of Misconduct by Company employees and Company agents are considered confidential and shall be maintained in a secure location for a minimum of ten years from the date of the Report, after which the information may be destroyed unless it is relevant to any pending or potential litigation, inquiry, or investigation in which case the information may not be destroyed and must be retained for the duration of that litigation inquiry, or investigation and thereafter as necessary.

7 Controlling/Monitoring

(a) Unless otherwise specified in this Policy, it is the responsibility of each local manager, department head and the Ethics Office to set up the necessary controls and processes to ensure the accurate respect of this Policy.

(b) The adherence of the procedures established in this Policy shall be supervised and monitored by the Ethics Office on a regular basis.

8 Violations—Reporting and Sanctioning

(a) Any violation of this Policy must be reported to the Ethics Office or the Company Compliance & Ethics Line.

(b) Violations of this Policy will result in disciplinary action up to and including termination of employment with the Company.

9 Approval / Amendments

(a) This Policy, as amended, is approved by the Corporate Governance Committee and the Audit Committee of the Company at its meeting of _____. This Policy enters into force on _____.

(b) Amendments to this Policy are only to be made by the Corporate Governance Committee and the Audit Committee of the Company.

10 Appendix

Reports of Misconduct relate to the following types of personal conduct by a Company employee or a Company agent:

Abuse of Ethics or other Hotline: the bad-faith use of the Company Compliance & Ethics Line or other reporting processes to harass a Company employee or Company agent or to file knowingly false information.

Competitive Issues: improper sales and marketing practices. This category includes allegations of unfair competition, unethical marketing practices, using a competitor's trade secrets, and making disparaging comments about competitors. An allegation of "unfair competition" includes discussing prices, strategies or sales terms with competitors. It also includes agreements covering customers or territories. This category also includes obtaining information about a competitor in some improper way.

Conflicts of Interest: a Company employee or Company agent made a decision while allowing their personal loyalties to conflict or appear to conflict with Company's interests. This category includes hiring or supervising a relative, having a financial, business or personal interest in a Company vendor or competitor, or having some outside personal interest which conflicts with Company's interests. This includes outside employment that creates a conflict of interest or diminishes productivity and effectiveness.

Confidential or Proprietary Information: a Company employee or Company agent improperly lost, used or possessed non-public information which Company is required to safeguard. This category includes software piracy, improper data copying, and the unauthorized use of a Company employee or Company agent's patent, copyright and trademark rights. This category includes the improper disclosure of Company business plans, pricing data, marketing programs, personnel information, and financial reports. This category also includes client-related confidential information.

Customer-site Incident: a Company employee or Company agent acted improperly at a customer location. This category includes on-site illegal activity, theft, vandalism and physical violence.

Employment Practices: a Company employee or Company agent acted improperly in the recruiting, hiring, assignment, evaluation, promotion, training, discipline or compensation of an employee. This category includes allegations of discrimination (race, color, gender, national origin, age, marital status, religion, disability, sexual orientation, veteran status or other status protected by applicable law).

Fraud: the improper accounting of business transactions, or not following internal accounting and financial-reporting rules, including (i) falsifying or forging financial records; (ii) the misstatement of expenses, revenues or business transactions; (iii) fraud or deliberate error in the preparation, review or audit of internal financial reports or statutory accounts; (iv) fraud or deliberate error in the recording and maintenance of the financial and corporate records of the Company; (v) false statements to investors, regulators, government authorities or members of the investing public; (vi) non-compliance with the Company's internal accounting controls, or other policies or procedures; (vii) misappropriation of Company assets, unlawful conduct toward employees in the workplace, violation of antitrust, anti-corruption, privacy or intellectual property laws; (viii) employee benefits fraud; (ix) corruption (i.e. bribery, extortion, kickbacks); (x) asset misappropriation (i.e. theft of Company assets, ghost employees, overstated expenses); and (xi) fraudulent statements (i.e. false employment credentials, false time records, false financial documentation).

Gifts, Gratuities and Entertainment: a Company employee or Company agent accepted something valuable, such as a gift, tickets or entertainment, from anyone who is trying to influence a business decision. The valuable item could be offered by a supplier, customer, supervisor or subordinate, or where the employee solicited the gift, ticket or entertainment. This includes where the gift-giver could seek or receive special favors from the colleague. This also includes entertainment that is not for bona fide business reasons.

Insider Trading and Securities Violations: a Company employee or Company agent knew non-public, material, Company-related information and then used that information in a stock transaction. "Non-public, material, Company-related information" includes financial results, earnings estimates, changes in management, major contract awards and potential acquisitions.

Internal Business Operations: some activity that conflicts with established Company business policies, procedures and practices. This category covers allegations that a Company employee or Company agent did not follow internal manuals, standard business practices or workplace health and safety procedures.

Internal Workplace Conduct: a Company employee or Company agent behaved improperly while on Company premises. This category includes harassment, threats, theft of property, offensive speech, improper employee relationships, and physical violence. This includes improper soliciting and distribution of material.

International Trade Controls: to improper actions in doing business outside the Home Country. ("Home Country" means the country in which the reported incident occurs.) This category export licenses, financial transactions, anti-boycott laws, offering or making improper payments to officials outside the Home Country.

Misuse of Internal Systems: a Company employee or Company agent improperly used the Company's telephone systems, computers, e-mail, voice mail, fax machines, teleconferencing services, copiers, internal data systems, or the Internet. This includes using the systems to send illegal, sexually explicit, abusive, offensive or profane messages. This also includes improperly uploading or downloading information. This also includes using the systems for soliciting funds or distributing information that is unrelated to Company business.

Money Laundering: a Company employee or Company agent, such as a vendor, tried to "launder" the proceeds of a crime—such as narcotics trafficking, bribery or fraud—in order to hide the money or make the amounts appear legitimate by making it look like a normal business transaction with the Company.

Political and Charitable Activities: a Company employee or Company agent made a payment to a political party, political organization, charity or an elected official that directly affects Company's business interests. This category includes participating in the activities of these organizations.

Purchasing: allegation relating to buying supplies or services for Company use. These allegations relate to how a vendor was chosen, the vendor's qualifications, or the price we were charged for the supplies or services.

Records and Document Retention: a Company employee or Company agent did not retain or safeguard Company books and records according to Company's document-retention guidelines. This category applies to the retention or destruction of Company documents in any form. This category includes destroying or concealing documents in order to avoid retention obligations.

Regulatory Noncompliance: a Company employee or Company agent did not follow a government rule or regulation. These rules and regulations include employee-verification requirements, visa and immigration rules, payroll and tax obligations, wage/ hour laws, labor-law violations, stock-exchange and other government rules.

Retaliation of Whistleblowers: a Company employee or Company agent who reported a possible ethics or compliance-related violation was treated unfairly because he made the report.

Substance Abuse: a Company employee or Company agent misused alcohol or drugs (legal or illegal) while at work. This category includes a Company employee or Company agent using prescription medication if that medication impaired that person's ability to do his or her job properly.

APPENDIX B

Sample Mission Statement

The mission of the Workplace Investigations Unit (the "WIU") is to provide the executive management of the company with a variety of coordinated investigation services. The goal of these services is to aid in accomplishing the WIU's primary purpose—improving the quality, efficiency and profitability of business processes.

It is the responsibility of the WIU to manage its own investigations and the company's investigation processes in an environment that respects and enforces proper conduct by employees. This allows for the appropriate correction of employee behavior that is not consistent with company values or policies.

Misconduct by these employees is vigorously investigated. This creates confidence among employees that their concerns will be taken seriously. The WIU coordinates these investigations to ensure that unit resources are used efficiently and productively.

The WIU is available to consult with other internal departments which are conducting employee-related investigations.

The WIU develops information regarding the identification of business risks and where business processes should be improved. This information is shared with key internal departments and executive management to help ensure that our customers receive the best possible services from the company.

The WIU is designated as the company's liaison with law-enforcement agencies in investigative and misconduct matters.

APPENDIX C

Corporate Compliance Department Notification Matrix for Key Internal Departments

As part of the Company's commitment to an ethical workplace and to ensure that the company meets its legal obligations, the Company requires colleagues and associates to report possible violations of the Company Code of Conduct. The company, through the Corporate Compliance Department ("Compliance"), responds to these reports. Compliance also tracks these incidents and reports them to the Board of Directors.

Compliance has primary responsibility to ensure that a detailed investigation of any possible misconduct has occurred. Compliance, therefore, depends on its colleagues in key internal departments to notify our group when these matters arise. These notifications are essential to allow Compliance to track the incident.

This matrix facilitates appropriate communication and interaction among the key internal departments that handle compliance-related matters. Each group, depending on the report, has an interest in the incident reported, its investigation, and its outcome. Proper implementation of the matrix ensures that each of these stakeholder groups learns about an incident when it arises.

The matrix is intended only to ensure appropriate notification. The matrix does not replace a business group's existing procedures for investigating these incidents. The matrix will allow our group to collaborate in investigations when it is appropriate for us to do so.

This matrix applies to possible ethics and compliance-related violations committed by Company directors and officers, colleagues, associates, and franchisees around the world. This matrix also applies to consultants, agents and independent contractors when they act on behalf of the Company.

The matrix follows this cover page. An "**X**" means that Compliance will notify this business group, if the business group is not already aware, once Compliance is notified that the incident has occurred.

Reported Incident	Business Unit	Senior Manager	Legal	Human Resources	Compliance
Abuse of Ethics or Other Hotline	X	X	X		X
Abuse or Fraud of Company Benefits	X		X		X
Accounting Irregularities	X	X	X		X
Branch Financial Violations	X	X			X
Competitive Issues	X		X		X
Conflicts of Interest	X		X		X
Confidential or Proprietary Information	X		X		X
Customer-site Incident	X	X	X	X	X
Employment Practices	X		X	X	X
Fraud	X	X	X		X
Gifts, Gratuities and Entertainment	X				X
Insider Trading and Securities Violations	X	X	X		X
Internal Business Operations	X	X	X		X
Internal Workplace Conduct	X		X	X	X
International Trade Controls	X	X	X		X
Kickbacks and Bribery	X	X	X		X
Misuse of Internal Systems	X		X	X	X
Money Laundering	X	X	X		X
Political and Charitable Activities	X		X		X
Purchasing	X	X			X
Records and Document Retention	X	X		X	X
Regulatory Noncompliance	X	X	X		X
Requests for Advice or Clarification (ethics issues only)	X				X
Requests for Assistance (employee-specific issues)	X			X	X
Retaliation of Whistleblowers	X	X	X		X
Substance Abuse	X		X	X	X

Note: Human Resources will be notified regardless of the Reported Incident category whenever an employee is likely to face any discipline, including possible termination.

Glossary

Business Unit means the internal business organization in which the incident arises. Notification is generally made to the immediate supervisor of the subject of the investigation.

Senior manager means both the senior senior manager and financial officers in the Home Country. This may also include the Risk Management and Internal-Audit staffs in the Home Country.

Home Country means the country in which the reported incident occurs.

Legal means the senior legal advisor in the Home Country.

Human Resources means the senior human-resources senior manager in the Home Country.

Compliance means the Corporate Compliance department.

* * *

Abuse of Ethics or other Hotline means an allegation relating to the bad-faith use of the compliance hotline or other reporting processes to harass someone or to file knowingly false information.

Accounting Irregularities means an allegation relating to the improper accounting of business transactions, or not following internal accounting and financial-reporting rules. This includes falsifying or forging financial records. This includes the misstatement of expenses, revenues or business transactions. (This does not include branch-level transactions, which are included in "Branch Financial Violations.")

Branch Financial Violations means an allegation that someone working in a branch or local office did not follow established procedures for handling financial processes, such as workers-compensation coding, wage/hour issues or handling past-due accounts. This includes the misstatement of branch expenses, branch revenues, or branch-level transactions. (This category does not include an allegation relating to financial reporting which is not on the branch level.)

Competitive Issues means an allegation relating to improper sales and marketing practices. This category includes allegations of unfair competition, unethical marketing practices, using a competitor's trade secrets, and making disparaging comments about competitors. An allegation of "unfair competition" includes discussing prices, strategies or sales terms with competitors. It also includes agreements covering customers or territories. This category also includes obtaining information about a competitor in some improper way.

Conflicts of Interest means an allegation that someone made a decision while allowing their personal loyalties to conflict or appear to conflict with the Company's interests. This category includes hiring or supervising a relative, having a financial, business or personal interest in a company vendor or competitor, or having some outside personal interest which conflicts with the Company's interests. This includes outside employment that creates a conflict of interest or diminishes productivity and effectiveness.

Confidential or Proprietary Information means an allegation that someone improperly lost, used or possessed non-public information which Company is required to safeguard. This category includes software piracy, improper data copying, and the unauthorized use of someone's patent, copyright and trademark rights. This category includes the improper disclosure of the Company business plans, pricing data, marketing programs, personnel information, and financial reports. This category also includes client-related confidential information.

Customer-site Incident means an allegation that someone acted improperly at a client location. This category includes on-site illegal activity, theft, vandalism and physical violence. (This category does not apply to misconduct at company premises.)

Employment Practices means an allegation that someone acted improperly in the recruiting, hiring, assignment, evaluation, promotion, training, discipline or compensation of an employee. This category includes allegations of discrimination (race, color, gender, national origin, age, marital status, religion, disability, sexual orientation, veteran status or other protected category).

Fraud means an allegation that someone deceived the company or someone else for personal gain. This category includes abuse of employee benefits and expense-report fraud. This category includes falsifying or forging business records other than financial records. This category includes embezzlement and mishandling of company funds.

Gifts, Gratuities and Entertainment means an allegation that someone accepted something valuable, such as a gift, tickets or entertainment, from anyone who is trying to influence an Company business decision. The valuable item could be offered by a supplier, customer, supervisor or subordinate, or where the employee solicited the gift, ticket or entertainment. This includes where the gift-giver could seek or receive special favors from the colleague. This also includes entertainment that is not for bona fide business reasons.

Insider Trading and Securities Violations means an allegation that someone knew non-public, material, Company-related information and then used that information in a stock transaction. "Non-public, material, Company-related information" includes financial results, earnings estimates, changes in management, major contract awards and potential acquisitions.

Internal Business Operations means an allegation relating to some activity that conflicts with established Company business policies, procedures and practices. This category covers allegations that someone did not follow internal manuals, standard business practices or workplace health and safety procedures. (This category does not cover legal, regulatory or accounting violations.)

Internal Workplace Conduct means an allegation that someone behaved improperly while on Company premises. This category includes harassment, threats, theft of property, offensive speech (not using an internal system), improper employee relationships, and physical violence. This includes improper soliciting and distribution of material. (Allegations relating to discrimination are included in "Employment Practices.")

International Trade Controls means an allegation relating to improper actions in doing business outside the Home Country. This category export licenses, financial transactions, anti-boycott laws, offering or making improper payments to officials outside the Home Country.

Kickbacks and Bribery means an allegation that someone made an improper or illegal payment to someone in the Home Country to influence the recipient's business decisions. This category includes offering, paying or accepting a bribe.

Misuse of Internal Systems means an allegation that someone improperly used the Company's telephone systems, computers, e-mail, voice mail, fax machines, teleconferencing services, copiers, internal data systems, or the Internet. This includes using the systems to send illegal, sexually explicit, abusive, offensive or profane messages. This also includes improperly uploading or downloading information. This also includes using the systems for soliciting funds or distributing information that is unrelated to company business.

Money Laundering means an allegation that someone, such as a vendor, tried to "launder" the proceeds of a crime—such as narcotics trafficking, bribery or fraud—in order to hide the money or make the amounts appear legitimate by making it look like a normal business transaction with the Company.

Political and Charitable Activities means an allegation that someone made a payment to a political party, political organization, charity or an elected official that directly affects the Company's business interests. This category includes participating in the activities of these organizations. (This category does not include someone's personal political or charitable activities that have no connection to the Company.)

Purchasing means an allegation relating to buying supplies or services for company use. These allegations relate to how a vendor was chosen, the vendor's qualifications, or the price we were charged for the supplies or services.

Records and Document Retention means an allegation that someone did not retain or safeguard company books and records according to the Company's document-retention guidelines. This category applies to the retention or destruction of company documents in any form. This category includes destroying or concealing documents in order to avoid retention obligations.

Regulatory Noncompliance means an allegation that someone did not follow a government rule or regulation. These rules and regulations include employee-verification requirements, visa and immigration rules, payroll and tax obligations, wage / hour laws, labor-law violations, stock-exchange and other government rules. (This category does not apply to failures to follow internal business procedures because those procedures are not required by the government. This category also does not include falsifying or forging financial records, and those are included in "Accounting Irregularities" or "Branch Financial Violations.")

Requests for Advice or Clarification means a request by someone for help understanding an ethics or compliance rule under the Code of Business Conduct before that person takes any action.

Requests for Assistance means a request by someone for help resolving an issue that would usually be handled by Human Resources or another business group, but was reported to Compliance.

Retaliation of Whistleblowers means the allegation that someone who reported a possible ethics or compliance-related violation was treated unfairly because he made the report.

Substance Abuse means an allegation that someone misused alcohol or drugs (legal or illegal) while at work. This category includes someone using prescription medication if that medication impaired that person's ability to do his or her job properly.

APPENDIX D

Highly Confidential

Memo

To: John Smith
From:
Date: January 1, 2007
Subject: New Internal Investigation—Case #000
Chicago, Illinois

    I write to inform you that an issue for workplace investigation has been brought to our attention. Based on the preliminary information we have, the allegation concerns improper workplace conduct at the _____ branch.

    Under our Management Notification Matrix, I am notifying you of this new pending investigation because the nature of the allegation impacts some of your department's responsibilities. I will be contacting employees in this office and in other departments in order to gather the necessary facts and determine whether this allegation can be substantiated. The scope of the investigation or the particular investigation subjects may change as the investigation progresses.

    Please know that, regardless of the allegation, no one is presumed to have acted improperly, unethically or in violation of company rules unless the investigation proves otherwise. No conclusions will be made until all the facts have been reviewed.

    If you choose, you may participate in the investigation process with me. Additionally, I may call upon you for specific information and/or to obtain relevant documents. I will make sure to update you as the investigation proceeds. As always, please maintain the confidentiality of this allegation and the subsequent investigation.

    Please feel free to contact me at (___) ___-_____ with any questions.

APPENDIX E

Corporate Compliance Department Colleague Referral Guidelines

As part of the company's commitment to an ethical workplace and to ensure that the company meets its legal obligations, the company encourages colleagues and associates, subject to local restrictions and guidelines, to report possible violations of business conduct. The company, through its Corporate Compliance Department ("Compliance"), responds to these reports. Compliance also tracks these incidents and reports them to the Board of Directors.

Compliance has primary responsibility to ensure that a detailed investigation of any possible violation has occurred. Compliance, therefore, depends on its colleagues in key internal departments to notify our group when these matters arise. These notifications are essential to allow Compliance to track the incident.

These guidelines are intended only to ensure that Compliance learns that the incident has occurred. **These guidelines do not replace a business group's existing procedures for investigating these incidents.** However, following the guidelines will allow our group to collaborate in investigations when it is appropriate for us to do so.

You will be expected to investigate an allegation of misconduct if it meets each of these requirements:

1. The report is made by an associate, colleague or third-party acting in good faith who genuinely believes that misconduct may have occurred.
2. The report relates to possible associate or colleague misconduct, and the report does not solely relate to a personnel-management issue.
3. On the face of the facts given by the reporter, the manager believes that misconduct may have occurred.

4. It is determined that the relevant facts of the suspected misconduct—regardless of how the reporter characterizes them—fall within one of these incident categories.

Please contact Compliance if you learn of an allegation that an associate, colleague or franchisee may have been involved in any of these:

Accounting Irregularities: the improper accounting of business transaction, or not following internal accounting and financial-reporting rules. This includes falsifying or forging financial records, or misstating expenses, revenues or business transactions.
Branch Financial Violations: someone working in a branch or local office did not follow established financial procedures for handling financial processes, such as workers-compensation coding, wage/hour issues or handling past-due accounts.
Competitive Issues: improper sales and marketing practices such as unfair competition, unethical marketing practices, and making disparaging comments about competitors. An allegation of "unfair competition" includes discussing prices, strategies or sales terms with competitors. It also includes agreements covering customers or territories. This category also includes obtaining competitor information in some improper way.
Conflicts of Interest: someone made a business decision while allowing their personal loyalties to conflict or appear to conflict with the company's interests. This includes hiring or supervising a relative, having a business or personal interest in a company vendor or competitor, or having some outside personal interest that conflicts with the company's interests. This also includes outside employment that creates a conflict of interest.
Confidential or Proprietary Information: someone improperly lost, used or possessed information which the company is required to safeguard. This includes software piracy, improper data copying, and unauthorized use of someone's copyright or trademark rights. This also includes the improper disclosure of the company business plans, pricing data, marketing programs, personnel information, financial reports, and client-related information.
Customer-site Incident: someone acted improperly at a client location. This includes on-site illegal activity, theft, vandalism and physical violence.

Employment Practices: someone acted improperly in the recruiting, hiring, evaluation, promotion, training, discipline or compensation of an employee. This includes discrimination (race, color, gender, national origin, age, marital status, religion, disability, sexual orientation, veteran status or other protected category).

Fraud: someone deceived the company or someone else for personal gain. This includes abuse of employee benefits and expense-report fraud. This includes falsifying business records, as well as embezzlement or mishandling of company funds.

Gifts, Gratuities and Entertainment: someone accepted something valuable, such as a gift, tickets or entertainment, from anyone trying to influence a company business decision. The valuable item could be offered by a supplier, customer, supervisor or subordinate, or if the employee solicited the gift, ticket or entertainment. This also includes entertainment that is not for bona fide business reasons.

Insider Trading and Securities Violations: someone knew non-public, material, The company-related information and then used that information in a stock transaction. "Non-public, material, company-related information" includes financial results, earnings estimates, changes in executive management, major contract awards and potential acquisitions.

Internal Business Operations: some business activity that violates established company business policies, procedures and practices. This includes allegations that someone intentionally did not follow internal manuals, standard business practices, or workplace health and safety procedures.

Internal Workplace Conduct: someone behaved improperly while on company premises. This includes harassment, threats, theft of property, offensive speech (not using an internal system), improper employee relationships, and physical violence. This includes improper soliciting and distribution of material.

International Trade Controls: someone acted improperly in order to do company business in another country. This includes export licenses, financial transactions, anti-boycott laws, offering or making improper payments to officials in the other country.

Kickbacks and Bribery: someone made an improper or illegal payment to someone for company business that is intended to influence the recipient's business decisions. This includes offering, paying or accepting a bribe.

Misuse of Internal Systems: someone improperly used the company's telephone systems, voice mail, fax machines, computers, e-mail, teleconferencing services, copiers, internal data systems, or the Internet. This includes using the systems to send illegal, sexually explicit, abusive, offensive or profane messages. This also includes improperly uploading or downloading information. This also includes using company systems for soliciting funds or distributing information that is unrelated to company business.

Money Laundering: someone, such as a vendor, tried to "launder" the proceeds of a crime—such as narcotics trafficking, bribery or fraud—in order to hide the money or make the amounts appear legitimate by making it look like a normal business transaction with the company.

Political and Charitable Activities: someone made a payment to a political party, charity, political organization or an elected official that directly affects The company's business interests. This includes participating in the activities of that organization. (This does not apply to someone's personal political or charitable activities that have no effect on the company's business.)

Purchasing: someone acted improperly when buying supplies or services for company use. The allegation relates to how a vendor was chosen, the vendor's qualifications, or the price we were charged for the supplies or services.

Records and Document Retention: someone did not retain or safeguard company books and records according to the company's document-retention guidelines. This applies to the retention or destruction of company documents. This includes destroying or concealing documents in order to avoid retention requirements.

Regulatory Noncompliance: someone did not follow a government rule or regulation. These rules and regulations include employee-verification requirements, visa and immigration rules, payroll and tax obligations, wage/hour laws, labor-law violations, stock-exchange and other government rules.

Retaliation of Whistleblowers: someone who reported a possible ethics or compliance-related violation was treated unfairly because he made the report.

Substance Abuse: someone misused alcohol or drugs (legal or illegal) while at work. This includes someone using prescription medication if that medication impaired that person's ability to do his or her job properly.

APPENDIX F

Fraud Red Flags

All fraud must be hidden to be successful. When fraud is detected, therefore, it is more likely to be noticed because of a "red flag." This means there was some unusual fact or detail that caught the attention of the auditor, investigator or other person. Not every red flag means that there has been a fraud. It only means that further inquiries are needed.

Although people can be creative when it comes to committing a fraud, there are actually a limited number of fraud schemes that arise in the workplace. As a result, it is possible to list many of the red flags for which auditors and investigators should be alert.

1 Red flags that show a corporate structure at risk for fraud
- Autocratic management style.
- Management style that is focused on profits.
- Management by crisis and with little employee trust.
- Bureaucratic management structure that is inflexible and with imposed controls.
- Management structure that has many tiers and is vertically controlled.
- Corporate authority is centralized and reserved for top management.
- Authority rules are rigidly enforced.
- Corporate planning is centralized and short-range.
- Performance is measures quantitatively and on a short-term basis.
- Management is primarily concerned with the preservation of capital and maximizing profits.
- The reward system can be punitive, politically administered and mainly monetary.
- External relationship with competitors and others is hostile.
- There are financial concerns about cash-flow shortages.
- The organization has a sporadic growth pattern.

2   **Red flags that show a corporate culture at risk for fraud**
    - The organization is ambivalent about business ethics.
    - The organization's values and beliefs are economic, political and self-centered.
    - Peer relationships are hostile, aggressive and contentious.
    - There is high employee turnover as well as complaints about "burnout."
    - There are inadequate job rewards: pay, fringe benefits, recognition, job security, and job responsibility.
    - There is ambiguity in defining job rules, duties and areas of responsibility.
    - There is a failure to counsel and take administrative action when performance or behavior standards are not met.
    - There are inadequate operational reviews.
    - There is general job-related stress and anxiety.
    - There is a failure to monitor and enforce policies on honesty, loyalty and fairness.

3   **Personality traits of executives who have a high potential to commit workplace fraud**
    - These managers tend to have highly material personal values.
    - Success to these managers means financial success, not professional recognition.
    - These managers tend to treat people as objects, not individuals and often as objects for exploitation.
    - These managers highly self-centered.
    - These managers often eccentric in the way they display their wealth or spend their money.
    - These managers tend to be conspicuous consumers and often boast of the things they have acquired, the friends they have in high office, and all the fine places they have visited.
    - These managers speak about their cunning achievements and winnings more than their losses.
    - These managers appear to be reckless or careless with facts and often enlarge on them.
    - These managers appear to be hard working, almost compulsive, but most of their time at work is spent scheming and designing short cuts to get ahead or beat the competition.
    - These managers may gamble or drink a great deal.

- These managers buy expensive gifts for their families usually to compensate for spending so little time with them.
- These managers are hostile to people who oppose their views.
- These managers feel exempt from accountability and controls because of their station or position.
- These managers create a greet deal of turnover among their subordinates and often set off one subordinate against the other.
- These managers play favorites among subordinates, but the relationship can cool very quickly because a subordinate often falls from grace after one mistake, even an insignificant one.
- These managers manage by crisis more often than by objectives.
- These managers tend to drift with the times and have no long-range plans, tend to override internal controls with impunity and argue forcefully for less formality in controls.
- These managers demand absolute loyalty from subordinates, but they themselves are loyal only to their own self-interests.
- These managers have few real friends within their own industry or company.
- These managers' competitors and colleagues often dislike them.

4 Red flags that show fraud may have already occurred

Discrepancies in Accounting Records
- Account balances that are significantly over or understated
- Transactions not recorded in a complete or timely manner or improperly recorded as to amount, accounting period, classification, or company policy
- Unsupported or unauthorized records, balances, or transactions
- Last-minute adjustments that significantly affect financial results (particularly those increasing income presented after submission of the proposed audit adjustments)

Conflicting or Missing Evidential Matter
- Missing documents
- Unexplained items on reconciliations
- Unavailability of other than photocopied documents
- Inconsistent, vague or implausible responses arising from inquiries or analytical procedures

- Unusual discrepancies between the client's records and confirmation replies
- Missing inventory or physical assets
- Excessive voids or credits
- Common names or addresses of payees or customers
- Alterations on documents (e.g. back dating)
- Duplications (e.g., duplicate payments)
- Questionable handwriting on documents
- Unusual relationships with the client
- The internal auditor is denied access to records or facilities
- The internal auditor is denied access to certain employees, customers, vendors, or others from whom audit evidence might be sought
- Undue time pressures imposed by management to resolve complex or contentious issues
- Unusual delays in providing requested information
- Tips or complaints to us about fraud
- Significant internal control weaknesses or prior year internal control weaknesses not corrected
- Unusual transactions (e.g., for activities outside the normal line of business)
- Changes in accounting principles or the methods of applying them that enhances reported income
- Departure of key financial or operating personnel
- Specific instances of management's conduct that raise serious concerns as to their integrity

Accounts Payable Process
- Recurring identical amounts from the same vendor.
- Unusual even dollar or high cash disbursement amounts for routine odd dollar or low value purchase.
- Multiple remittance addresses for the same vendor.
- Vendor addresses do not agree with vendor approval application.
- Sequential invoice numbers from the same vendor or invoice numbers with an alpha suffix.
- Payments to vendor have increased dramatically for no apparent reason.
- Lack of segregation of duties between the following:
- Processing of accounts payable invoice and updates to vendor master files

- Check preparation and posting to vendor account
- Check preparation and mailing of signed checks
- No proper documentation of additions, changes, or deletions to vendor master file.
- Excessive credit adjustments to a particular vendor and/or credit issued by unauthorized department (credits involving quantities and price).
- Systematic pattern of adjustments to accounts payable for goods returned.
- No reconciliation performed of accounts payable subledger to general ledger control account.
- Insufficient supervisory review of accounts payable activity.
- Lack of documentation for payment of invoices.
- Cash disbursements for unrecorded liabilities and routine expenses (e.g., rent) when all expenditures must be vouchered prior to payment.
- Excessive miscodings to same expense account.
- Payments made on copies of invoices, not originals.
- Paid invoices not properly canceled, allowing for reprocessing.
- High volume of manually prepared disbursement checks.
- Unrestricted access to blank checks, signature plates, and check-signing equipment.
- Missing or easy access to blank checks, facsimile, and manual check preparation machines.
- Vendor invoices are received by department other than accounts payable (purchasing).
- Vendor complaints noted by credit rating services regarding slow or no payments not justified by disbursement schedule.

Purchasing Process
- Turnover among buyers within the purchasing department significantly exceeds attrition rates throughout the organization.
- Purchase order proficiency rates fluctuate significantly among buyers within comparable workload levels.
- Dramatic increase in purchase volume by certain vendor(s) not justified by competitive bidding or changes in production specifications.
- Unaccounted purchase order numbers or physical loss of purchase orders.

- Rise in the cost of routine purchases beyond the inflation rate.
- Unusual purchases not consistent with the categories identified by prior trends or operating budget.

Payroll Process
- Dramatic increase in labor force or overtime not justified by production or sales volume.
- Turnover within the payroll department significantly exceeds attrition rates throughout the organization.
- Missing or easy access to blank checks, facsimile, and manual check preparation machine.
- Tax deposits are substantially less than those required by current payroll expenses.
- High volume of manually prepared payroll checks.

Cash Receipts Process
- Improper safeguarding of cash under lock and key.
- No segregation of duties between the following:
- Discrepancies in receiving cash and posting to customer accounts
- Consistent shortages in cash on hand.
- Consistent fluctuations in bank account balances.
- Excessive number of voided transactions on a regular basis without proper explanation.
- Missing copies of pre-numbered receipts.
- Not balancing cash to accounts receivable subledger.
- Insufficient supervisory review of cashier's daily activity.

Accounts Receivable Process
- Lack of accountability for invoice numbers issued.
- Lack of segregation of duties between the following:
  - Processing of accounts receivable invoices and posting to subledger
  - Posting to accounts receivable subledger and cash receipts
- Lack of policies and procedures regarding write-offs to satisfy industry standards.
- Frequent undocumented and/or unapproved adjustments, credits, and write—offs to accounts receivable subledger.
- Low turnover or slow collection cycle for accounts receivable.
- Dramatic increase in allowance for doubtful accounts in view of positive economic events and stringent credit policies.

- No reconciliation of accounts receivable subledger to general ledger control account.
- Insufficient supervisory review of accounts receivable activity as well as customer account aging schedule.
- Unrestricted access to subledgers and general ledger.

Finance Process
- Significant adjustments to accrued liabilities, accounts receivable, contingencies, and other accounts prior to acquisition of new financing.
- Dramatic change in key leverage, operating, and profitability ratios prior to obtaining financing.
- Adopting a change in accounting principle or revising an accounting estimate prior to obtaining financing.
- Increase in short-term cash and a decrease in receivables while sales are increasing prior to seeking new financing.
- A change in external activities, legal counsel, or treasury department head prior to obtaining new financing.
- A delay in issuance of monthly, quarterly, or annual financial reports prior to seeking new financing.

5 Red flags that may indicate a specific fraud scheme

Fraudulent financial statement red flags
- Management places undue emphasis on meeting earning projections or other quantitative targets.
- Management's attitude toward financial reporting is unduly aggressive.
- The client has a weak control environment.
- A substantial portion of management compensation depends on meeting quantified targets.
- Management's operating and financial decisions are dominated by a single person or a few persons acting in concert.
- Management displays a propensity to take undue risks.
- Key managers are considered unreasonable.
- The organization is decentralized without adequate monitoring.
- Management and/or key accounting personnel turnover is high.
- Client profitability is inconsistent with its industry.
- Unreasonable increase in gross margin.

- Recurring negative cash flows, especially when coupled with increasing profits.
- The client is confronted with adverse legal consequences.
- Management shows undue concern with the need to maintain or improve the image/reputation of the entity.
- There are adverse conditions in the client's industry or external environment.
- Client management is inexperienced.
- The client is in a period of rapid growth.
- The client is subject to significant contractual commitments.
- The client's operating results are highly sensitive to economic factors like inflation, unemployment, currency rates, etc.
- Significant, unusual or highly complex transactions at the end of the fiscal year.
- Excessive transfers from one entity to a related entity
- Vendor invoices or other liability transactions that are not recorded in the books.
- Unexplained or unusual increases in book value of assets.

Corruption schemes red flags
- A large volume of transactions with a particular vendor.
- The discovery of a relationship between an employee and a third party that was previously unknown.
- Weak segregation of duties in assigning contracts and approving invoices.
- A change in the lifestyle of a key management employee.

Asset-misappropriation schemes red flags
- Lower than expected revenues.
- Actual profits that are less than projections
- Gross margins that are less than projections.
- Customer complaints about payments being posted long after they sent a payment check in.
- Growing delinquency in accounts receivable or specific customers (shows that the payment is deposited but not posted right away).
- Unusual or unexplained drops in the level of bank deposits.
- Unusual or unexplained differences between the accounts or reports of activities and bank-statement information.

- Vendor who consistently gets paid more than other vendors.
- Notations for "extra" or "special" charges.
- A vendor who only bills for services.
- Unusual or unexpected increases in overhead costs.
- High prices are paid for certain products or services.
- Declining profits but increasing costs of goods sold.
- Amounts of invoices are just below an approval level, especially an excessive number of invoices below that number by a vendor or an employee who approved the transaction.
- Unusual or unexplained purchases of particular goods or services.
- Employees who never take vacation or time off.
- No follow-up procedures for missing time cards.
- No customer confirmation process with orders kept open.
- Poor segregation of branch-office duties between time approval and check receipt.
- Instructions to client and support to ensure against associate fraud.

APPENDIX G

Critical Event Reporting Policy

Purpose: This policy describes the procedures and guidelines for identifying and reporting information relating to critical events. It is in the best interests of the company to respond to these events quickly, decisively and in a coordinated manner.

Scope: This scope applies to all Company associates and colleagues within the United States and Canada.

Definitions of a Critical Event: A "critical event" is an occurrence arising outside the normal course of the Company's business operations and which, unless it is addressed properly, might expose the company to adverse legal, financial, public-relations or reputation risks. Each of the following should be considered a critical event under this policy:

- Suspected or actual criminal activity at a Company office
- Suspected or actual criminal activity by a Company employee whether at a Company office or on assignment at a client location
- Physical threats against or by a Company employees
- Any event that could or does result in serious injury or harm to a Company employees (such as an on-site personal accident, fire, or bomb threat)
- Fraud, abuse or unethical behavior by a Company employees or third parties with whom Company does business
- Inquiries or contacts by law enforcement officers or regulatory agencies
- Receipt of legal process or lawyer complaint letter (such as a subpoena, notice of hearing or investigation, judicial or administrative complaint)
- Contacts by members of the media

Reporting Procedures: Each Company permanent or temporary employee is expected to use reasonable discretion to determine whether a critical event has occurred. If, for some reason, an employee is unable to determine precisely whether a critical event has occurred, the employee should report the event anyway.

When a critical event occurs, there is a short period of time following the identification of then event by which the company must respond to avoid adverse consequences. Critical events will be reported to a designated company telephone number within *two* hours after either the event occurred or the person who makes the report learned of the event. The telephone number is (___) ___-____.

This telephone number is NOT a 911 or emergency service. Do not call this number to report events presenting an immediate threat to life and property. Reports submitted by calling this number may not receive an immediate response.

Management Response: The report will be directed to the appropriate member of executive management for handling. The reporter will be contacted for additional information and to assist, where appropriate, in responding to the matter.

After the matter is handled, a written report may be prepared to document the critical event in order to identify ways in which business processes might be improved.

This policy is not intended to change any other policy or procedure regarding how such events are to be handled within the company. Reporting a critical event under this policy, for example, does not relieve an employee from contacting his or her supervisor. Accordingly, this policy should be followed in addition to any other Company policy or procedure applies to the situation.

Effective date: _____

APPENDIX H

Memo

To: Outside Counsel
From:
Date:
Subject: Guidelines for Misconduct Investigations

The Corporate Compliance Department (*"Compliance"*) implements and oversees legal-compliance and comprehensive business-ethics programs throughout the company. The Code of Conduct applies to all employees. From time to time, circumstances arise within the conduct of the Company's business that lead to allegations of misconduct by an employee of the company, or a potential violation of law or regulation.

Referrals

It is the Company's policy to investigate thoroughly all allegations of legal or ethical misconduct. The investigation process is conducted in a manner that treats those affected with dignity and fairness.

When Compliance learns of an allegation of possible legal or ethical misconduct, we review the matter to determine whether an investigation is required. If so, we will open an investigation of the matter. In many instances, we conduct the investigation in-house, without the assistance of outside counsel. We conduct the investigation according to our specified investigation protocol which applies to all company investigations.

Under certain circumstances, it is appropriate to have the matter investigated by outside counsel. Regardless of whether the investigation is conduct internally or by outside counsel, however, each investigation should follow the same standards to ensure the confidentiality, objectivity and impartiality of the investigation. This will help to ensure that the investigation is adequately documented if the company must later defend how the investigation was conducted.

Your investigation should, to the extent possible, preserve the company's attorney-client privilege. Your findings should make clear that the investigation is for the purpose of providing legal advice to the company and, if appropriate under the circumstances, is being conducted in anticipation of litigation.

When we refer a matter to outside counsel for investigation, we will define for you the scope of that investigation based on the information available at that time. Generally, the scope of the investigation will be to determine (i) whether the particular allegation(s) can be substantiated by the facts elicited during the investigation, and (ii) to identify relevant areas for the improvement of the operations, efficiency or effectiveness of the department involved. (For example, an investigation may find that there is ineffective management supervision, insufficient training or the lack of a needed corporate policy.) Your investigation should not be conducted simply to uncover sufficient facts to determine if misconduct occurred.

The Company uses the findings of its workplace investigations to improve our business, either by identifying areas of unacceptable business risk or flawed business operations which expose the company needlessly. The business goals of the investigation include any of the following:

- Minimizing business risk.
- Identifying weaknesses in business operations.
- Removing certain individuals from the company.
- Recovering company assets that were lost because of the misconduct.
- Obtaining the criminal prosecution of those involved.
- Protecting the company's public image and reputation.
- Preparing for anticipated civil or criminal litigation involving the company.

Information developed from an investigation maximizes options for those managers who must decide on the solution. We partner with our management to identify and quantify risks to our business.

The company's standard investigation protocol is specified in the "Guide to Conducting Investigations." This protocol should be followed unless you determine that some valid reason exists to deviate from it. A copy of the guide is attached to this memorandum.

Interviews and Documents

Investigations will often involve interviewing Company employees and those temporary employees assigned to work for the Company's customers. The person being interviewed should be treated with dignity and fairness. The integrity of our workplace investigation process and the perception among employees that the process is fair is critically important to our business goals.

At the beginning of the interview, the interviewer should describe in general terms the nature and purpose of the interview. The interviewer should also read our "Instructions for Witnesses" document to the witness. A copy of the document is attached to this memorandum.

Please invite the witness to submit a written personal statement of the relevant facts if the witness wishes to do so. Please ensure that the statement is signed and dated. The statement should be added to the investigation file.

Please draft an interview memorandum shortly after the interview. This memorandum should specify exactly what happened in the interview, including direct quotes and any admissions. Once the memorandum has been drafted, any handwritten notes or other documentation about the interview should be destroyed so that there is only one statement of what transpired at the interview. You may retain the memorandum in your investigation file unless you believe it is important to share that information with us earlier.

We will assist you to obtain any company documents you believe are relevant to the investigation. We may also designate other company contacts, such as a member of Human Resources, to assist you.

Written Report

Once you have completed your fact finding, please prepare a written report of the results of the investigation. You may also offer recommendations about proposed corrective action. A template document is attached to this memorandum for your use.

We use written reports to assist management to develop corrective procedures to avoid repetitions of questionable conduct. We also use the reports, where necessary, to communicate to third parties that wrongful conduct did not occur or that corrective action has been taken internally.

Please do not offer any recommendations about possible disciplinary action against specific employees because this is outside the scope of the investigation. To ensure consistent administration of sanctions across the company, disciplinary action is handled internally by our Human Resources department and the relevant business unit management. Similarly, please do not offer any recommendations regarding whether the Company should compensate someone.

In order to preserve the attorney-client privilege, the report should be marked confidential, and the report should be distributed only to us.

Possible Problems

During the course of your investigation, certain problems may arise. We address some of them here to recommend how they should be handled on our behalf.

Company policy and applicable law protect whistleblowers and similar persons against retaliation for reporting incidents of possible or actual misconduct. It is absolutely prohibited for any person who participates in a company investigation to be penalized in any manner because of their participation. Please contact us immediately if you have reason to believe that any form of retaliation may have occurred or may be threatened.

You may not compel any person to submit to an interview during the investigation. As an employer, the Company may have certain recourse against such an employee for their refusal to submit to the interview. Therefore, if an employee refuses, please inform the employee that you will not force the employee to be interviewed, and that you will refer the issue to us to address the matter with the witness' superiors. Please contact us as soon as possible after the meeting.

During the course of an interview, your fact-finding may uncover additional facts which may indicate that additional violations or more-serious misconduct has occurred. Similarly, you may believe that your investigation should be expanded to include additional investigation subjects. If you uncover such facts, please contact us immediately to discuss the matter. Please do not expand the scope of your investigation without discussing it with us first.

Employees may ask you whether they are in trouble or whether they will be disciplined. Be straightforward—it is certainly possible that employees may be disciplined if they engage in misconduct, but please emphasize that your role in the investigation is to determine the true facts so management may be advised accordingly. Never represent to a witness that the company may consider their cooperation to be a quid pro quo for avoiding any disciplinary, civil or criminal action.

A witness may ask if he needs the assistance of a lawyer. This poses a problem that requires an immediate response. While everyone has the right to consult an attorney, the Company has the right to require its employees to disclose information that is relevant to the company's business. Please offer no opinion on whether the witness needs a lawyer. Please remind the witness that you are representing the company and cannot provide the witness with any legal advice. (Your notes should state the substance of this exchange during the interview.) The Company is not required to allow interview subjects to have a lawyer present and can insist that the interview continue with the witness without a lawyer present. If this situation arises, please contact us to discuss further steps.

An employee may ask if her she may have a co-worker present during the interview. We generally accommodate these requests if (i) the co-worker has no connection to the matter under investigation, and (ii) the co-worker does not interfere with the questioning or the answers offered by the witness. However, you may, at your discretion, decline the request if you believe that it would negatively impact the interview.

At the beginning of an investigation and at various points during its course, you should make a good-faith assessment whether the matter under investigation poses the risk of criminal liability for the company or any of the employees. If so, inform the witness of the option to retain personal counsel and have the personal counsel present during the interview. If requested, be prepared to postpone or suspend the interview long enough to permit the witness to obtain counsel or consider whether to do so.

Please contact us immediately if you believe that, for some reason, the company should take some interim action pending the completion of the investigation, such as the suspension of an employee or the seizure of documents and equipment. The Company will take whatever steps are reasonably necessary to protect the safety of our employees and to protect the integrity of the company's policies and procedures.

If you believe during the investigation, that any criminal activity may have occurred, please contact us immediately. Unless there is some immediate risk, do not contact any law-enforcement agency without our prior consent and participation.

APPENDIX I

Memo

To: John Smith
From:
Date: January 1, 2007
Subject: New Internal Investigation—Case #000
Chicago, Illinois

I write to inform you that an issue for workplace investigation has been brought to our attention. Based on the preliminary information we have, the allegation concerns improper workplace conduct by _____, a member of the branch staff.

I am notifying you of this new pending investigation because the allegation pertains to an office within your territory. I will be contacting employees in this office and in other departments in order to gather the necessary facts and determine whether this allegation can be substantiated. The scope of the investigation or the particular investigation subjects may change as the investigation progresses.

Please know that, regardless of the allegation, no one is presumed to have acted improperly, unethically or in violation of company rules unless the investigation proves otherwise. No conclusions will be made until all the facts have been reviewed.

You may be called upon to assist me in conducting the investigation by facilitating certain interviews and/or obtaining relevant documents. I will make sure to update you as the investigation proceeds. As always, please maintain the confidentiality of this allegation and the subsequent investigation.

Please feel free to contact me at (___) ___-____ with any questions.

APPENDIX J

Conducting Workplace Investigations

Many companies, in addition to codes of ethics and conduct, have found it necessary to create investigation guidelines to assist employees from various corporate backgrounds—law, human resources, audit, finance, etc.—to conduct workplace investigations.

In the current business environment, how companies investigate potential misconduct can affect that company's reputation almost as much as the alleged conduct itself. Consistent principles and procedures must be followed whenever allegations of misconduct are investigated.

Few people in a corporation are trained investigators. Even if you have business experience conducting interviews and obtaining information from employees and others, you may not have actively participated in many workplace investigations. The techniques and goals of these investigations are often different.

This guide gives you information and practical advice on how to handle an investigation effectively. It is true that every workplace investigation will have unique issues, circumstances, dimensions, challenges and outcomes. But an investigation can cause serious harm if it is not conducted properly.

Following the guide ensures that each of our investigations is conducted in a professionally consistent manner and will yield the best results. These guidelines should be viewed as the umbrella standard for a workplace investigation within the company.

The Reasons for an Internal Investigation

A workplace investigation is conducted when there is credible information there may have been significant wrongdoing, misconduct or ethical lapses. An workplace investigation may also be appropriate even if there have not been specific allegations against an employee or department, but there have been allegations against others, and the investigation is intended to exclude the possibility that wrongdoing occurred within the company.

An effective investigation process protects the interests of the Company and its shareholders by (i) preventing and detecting misconduct and violations; (ii) ensuring that corporate activities comply with applicable laws and regulations; and (iii) identifying areas of improvement for internal business operations. Therefore, an investigation is not conducted simply to uncover sufficient facts to justify a result or to just record somewhere that the incident occurred.

An investigation is, in the first instance, fact-finding. Investigations determine, fully and credibly, what happened with respect to a particular incident—whether suspected conduct did or did not take place; what the circumstances were; who was involved; whether a violation of law or company policy occurred. An investigation must be perceived as having been thorough, independent and analytical.

The Request from Compliance

The Company's Corporate Compliance Department ("Compliance") has primary responsibility to ensure that incidents of actual or suspected violations of the Code of Conduct (the "Code") are properly investigated. The investigation usually begins with a report of a possible Code violation to the Company Compliance and Ethics Line. Sometimes, a possible Code violation may be reported to us by another business unit.

Colleagues in key internal departments may learn of an incident when they are contacted by The Company associates or colleagues in the field. Some of these incidents need to be reported to Compliance. For specific guidelines for your department regarding the incidents to be reported to Compliance, please consult the attachments to this guide.

Once received by Compliance, the matter is reviewed by the Investigations Manager. The Investigations Manager is responsible for developing the investigation process and monitoring all workplace investigations, regardless of the internal department actually conducting the investigation.

The Investigations Manager makes a threshold determination whether a formal investigation is needed. Some problems reported to Compliance may be resolved quickly and informally without an investigation. If no investigation is warranted, the reporter is contacted and the matter is referred to colleagues in other business units. For example, reports received by the hotline are routinely referred to Human Resources when they involve personnel-management issues.

If warranted, an investigation of the report is opened, and the relevant corporate management is informed. Until the report has been proven or a suspicion validated, however, there is no confirmation of wrongdoing.

The Investigations Manager then reviews the report and may gather some preliminary information for the investigative plan. The investigative plan identifies and lists the questions that must be answered in order to determine whether the report can be substantiated. The plan will also identify the likely sources of information needed to answer those questions.

The investigation plan also sets the scope of the investigation. This is a critical component and corresponds to the severity of the matter under investigation. The scope also focuses on the business processes, company practices and other business-related issues. Personal interviews and document reviews are then generally limited to matters within the scope of the investigation.

I. Basic Principles

The Company's Board of Directors expects us to conduct a prompt, effective and thorough investigation. Without a reliable understanding of the facts, we cannot advise Company management of the consequences that may be expected to flow from the matter under investigation. Each investigator should observe each of these basic principles:

Confidentiality

Every aspect of an investigation should be kept confidential. Maintaining confidentiality is critical to the integrity of an investigation. There can be serious consequences for failing to ensure that confidentiality is maintained. These consequences include

- Damage to someone's reputation if others learn that the allegations were made.
- The success of the investigation can be undermined if others know of the investigation.
- The subject of the investigation could try to cover-up any misconduct if they learn they are being investigated.
- The company may face liability or negative publicity.

- The company's ability to defend any legal action associated with the matter could be compromised.
- The disclosure of the information could cause retaliatory action.

The need for confidentiality begins when the report is received. The fact that an investigation is underway, its subject matter, the processes followed, the materials gathered and, especially, the results of the investigation must always be treated confidentially. This includes being careful about the using the details of the investigation at a later time if the details could identify the person or the business department involved.

Proper Mindset

Doubt is one of the primary attributes of any investigator. Investigators must be appropriately skeptical. They should not assume that management or employees are honest and telling the whole truth until the facts are gathered and the inquiries are complete. They must have sufficient imagination to develop sufficient theories against which to compare factual evidence as it develops. They must persevere until the anomalies are resolved and the fact pattern is thoroughly understood. Finally, they must have patience to find the smallest detail that less-experienced people may overlook but that can provide that vital clue or inconsistency. Investigators discover the truth as a result of their ability to inquire and learn from that inquiry.

Professionalism

The essence of professionalism is that the investigators conduct the investigation with integrity, fairness and diligence. How the investigation is conducted reflects the professionalism of the company. Often the integrity of an investigation is judged by the reputation of the investigators. The way you conduct an interview, for example, sets the perception that you and the company take the investigation seriously, that you mean what you say, and that you will do what you say you will.

Acting with professionalism means treating everyone involved with respect. It also means that you ask for help when you need it. It is not a failure of professionalism to admit that you need guidance or other assistance to complete your investigation.

Independence

Both investigators and decision makers should protect the company and those who work for it. Investigators must be free from actual or apparent bias or conflict of interest. Consideration must be given to whether an investigator's judgment may be affected or criticized by previous biases or political considerations, whether real or not. For example, an in-house investigator should not investigate the conduct of his or her superiors. Also, in-house investigators who witnessed the underlying conduct should not participate in the workplace investigation.

Independence means that everyone gets a fair chance, and that all investigation subjects are each investigated in the same manner, with the same professional, impartial, objective treatment.

Competence

The quality of an investigation also depends on the competence of the investigators. The ability to investigate and interview effectively is an acquired skill. Investigators must have the experience and the expertise to conduct a credible investigation. Investigators must understand how to interview witnesses, manage documents and other records, and to maintain any applicable privileges to the extent possible. Investigators should also be fully informed about company policies, procedures and company history. Investigators must know the management controls and strategies employed by the relevant business unit. Investigators must be able to contribute to the discussion of risks to the business, highlighting potential likelihood or severity of risk areas.

The investigative team must also be mindful of the various legal and business implications of the investigation and the techniques used to gather evidence relevant to the allegations. Structuring an interview to obtain the most information possible, either through careful questioning or through exploiting the weaknesses in a witness' story requires substantial preparation and analysis of all available evidence. The company must consider whether the circumstances of the interview and the backgrounds of the witnesses in selecting the interviewer.

Objectivity and Impartiality

Throughout our lives, we develop our own set of values. These values influence the way we live and the decisions we make. These values are subjective. They are shaped in part by gender, by education, by race, by intellectual capacity, and by personal experience. But these have nothing to do with the reported conduct in an investigation which must be viewed objectively. All information must be reviewed and analyzed using the same standards, and the findings in an investigation should be based on the facts, not an opinion filtered through the investigator's personal value system. A good investigator always understands and factors in his or her own natural biases.

Preventing Retaliation

Those who report possible or actual misconduct and those who cooperate in an investigation must be protected from retaliation. An employee will only provide information to us if they believe that they will not be penalized for doing so. You need to be alert to signs of retaliation. It can occur at any time, not only after an incident is reported or an investigation is started.

Timeliness

Each investigation is unique in some way. There are varying levels of complexity and time requirements. But each investigation needs to be done promptly. Timeliness is certainly part of professionalism, but it is important for other reasons:

- Innocent people should be cleared as soon as possible.
- Corrective action is generally more effective when taken sooner.
- Continuing misconduct must be stopped as quickly as possible.

Best Practices

Investigating an allegation is equal parts of art and science. The techniques needed to investigate allegations of misconduct competently vary. However, a good investigation begins by following each of these practices:

- You must be fair and objective. Everyone involved in an investigation deserves to be treated with respect and dignity. Under typical circumstances, the subject will receive reasonable notice of the report and be offered a real opportunity to respond.
- Words have special meanings. The person who brings a matter to our attention is a "reporter." The report is not a complaint or claim. If the report is made regarding someone, that person is a "subject" of the investigation, not a target. Using proper terminology reinforces your role as a business-oriented truth gatherer.
- A common investigator error is to pre-judge the outcome of an investigation before all the witnesses have been interviewed

and all the relevant documents have been reviewed. Resist the temptation to jump to conclusions. It could cloud your judgment. Until the report has been proven or a suspicion validated, there is no confirmation of wrongdoing. Nor should a report be dismissed simply based on your opinion of the source. You should keep an open mind to other possible explanations or scenarios.
- You should be sensitive to any actual or perceived conflicts of interest that might arise. Investigations must avoid even the appearance of bias or partiality to a particular person or result. If you believe that an actual or perceived conflict exists—such as if you know the people involved in some way that might compromise his objectivity or you have some interest in the matter being investigated—you should stop and inform Compliance immediately.
- Keep the interviews serious and business-like. you should remain calm and in control throughout the interview. An interview is no place for joking, sarcasm or threats.
- A good investigator never stoops to undignified tactics. At times, you may need to be aggressive or tenacious, but never insulting or demeaning. There are times in an interview when you may not be treated politely. Despite the hurt and angry feelings such conduct may evoke, you cannot lower yourself to that level. If you become angry, insulted or offended during an interview, you give up control of the interview.
- You should never mislead a witness. This will result in employees distrusting the entire process—exactly the opposite atmosphere we are trying to create.
- You should not tell the witness what other witnesses had to say. You do not want the witness to conform his or her statements to the statements of others.
- You should not try to impress the witness. Your job is to obtain information, not give it out. Similarly, you should not reveal what you know about the relevant facts. If you do, you will also tell them what you do not know.
- You should not expect an admission in an interview. The investigation should focus instead on eliciting as much relevant information as possible.
- You should not discuss your opinions or conclusions. You should keep the witness guessing as to how much you actually know.

- You should interview only one person at a time, not groups of people at the same time. Group dynamics and peer pressure may distort or suppress responses.
- You should not tape-record the interview. Recording may have a chilling effect on the person being interviewed. While a taped account may maximize accuracy, the better approach is a more conversational format with one or two notetakers present. Thereafter, the interview notes can be reviewed and cross-checked to have an accurate account of the interview.
- The interview approach should be to facilitate a candid discussion. You should consider the comfort of the witness. You should conduct the interview occur at a place where the witness is comfortable and most likely to be forthcoming with information. You may consider whether an on-site interview may be inhibiting.
- Sometimes you will conduct the interview by telephone. If the person being interviewed puts you on hold, you should note the times. It may be related to a call the witness makes to another person while you are waiting.
- You must also protect the confidentiality of the investigation. Not every report is substantiated. Some investigations are closed without the need to discipline anyone involved. However, allegations of misconduct, even if later found to be groundless, can still damage someone's reputation. You should not disclose the allegations or the existence of an investigation to anyone who does not need to know. Curiosity by others, including executive management, is not a basis for sharing information about an investigation. The inadvertent disclosure of information could lead to the subject employee bringing claims for defamation or infliction of emotional distress.
- When considering who should be interviewed, please remember that an interview will result in the witness learning that there is an issue or concern relating to the facts discussed in the interview. You should impress upon them the need for confidentiality.
- Documents should be safeguarded against inadvertent disclosure. You should keep them in a secure place.
- You should make the inquiries promptly, but take the time needed to exercise appropriate diligence. You should make sure the inquiries are made timely to ensure that appropriate documents and e-mails are preserved, and that all steps are taken to stop continuing or imminent noncompliance.

- Every interview should identify, to the extent possible, the witness' personal biases and the basis of their knowledge of the operative facts. Each witness has some bias, and that bias is not fatal to the witness' recollection of facts. However, the interview must identify whether there is some personal feelings—animosity, friendship, anger, fear, etc.—which may color the witness's perceptions.
- Those participating in investigations should take all steps necessary to protect whistleblowers and those who cooperate in the investigation. You should avoid disclosing to the witness the source of the report. Any report of retaliation that emerges during the investigation should be treated as an additional report of possible misconduct and reported to the Investigations Counsel immediately.
- When making inquiries, you should consider the broader implications of what you have discovered for the affected business unit or the company as a whole. In addition to making recommendations to management about what, if any, action should be taken with regard to the person involved, you should recommend appropriate changes to policies, procedures, training, monitoring, audits, or other steps to prevent a recurrence. The investigation should be used as an opportunity to improve the business.

Business Goals of the Investigation

Properly conducted investigations improve the business, either by identifying areas of unacceptable business risk or flawed business operations which expose the company needlessly. you should have a clear idea from the outset about what the purposes of the investigation are and what the goals to be achieved are. The goals could be any of the following:

- Minimizing business risk.
- Identifying weaknesses in business operations.
- Removing certain individuals from the company.
- Recovering company assets that were lost because of the misconduct.
- Obtaining the criminal prosecution of those involved.
- Protecting the company's public image and reputation.
- Preparing for anticipated civil or criminal litigation involving the company.

Understanding your goals ensures that the investigation stays focused.

II. The Interview Process

Preparing for your Investigative Interview

Before you start asking questions, you need a plan. Without a plan, your inquiries will be ineffective. A poorly planned or ineffective investigation may actually be worse than no investigation at all.

Prepare an outline before the interview. What information does the witness have that you need? Careful planning will usually eliminate the need to re-interview people. A list of questions prepared before conducting an interview is a good basis for the interview. However, the list should serve only as a guide to ensure that all questions are asked. Please do not use an interview script. Remain flexible and attuned to what the witness says so that strategy can be changed if necessary.

Generally, you should inform a witness' immediate supervisor of the investigation and your intention to interview the witness. Ask the supervisor to be vigilant for further problems, retaliation or other reactions which may affect the situation.

The Difference between Interviews and Interrogations

But please remember that an interview is not an interrogation. The difference between the two is generally determined by the willingness of the person from whom you are to gain information. Interviews are generally taken with willing witnesses, those who are ready to tell you whatever they need to know. Simply put, the individual is willing to cooperate, and you need only to ask the questions for which they want answers.

On the other hand, the witness may be reluctant to provide the needed information, or to cooperate. In these situations, you have a two-step task: first, to make the subject willing to cooperate with the questioning, and secondly, to interview him. This is the challenge to you. There are a number of ways you can use to get a reluctant witness to cooperate:

- Ask general questions.
- Explain the advantages of cooperation.
- Downplay the disadvantages of non-cooperation.
- Play on their conscience.
- Speak their language and empathize.
- Give them a chance to explain.

Whatever the methods, the basic need for you is to develop a rapport with the witness. This creates a connection between you, and it then becomes possible to create a change in the behavior of the witness. The dynamics of rapport constitute the foundation of the inquiry-persuasion process. It allows you to enter the world of the witness.

Meeting the Reporter

You want the reporter to give you a complete account of the facts relating to the report. Please deal with the reporter in such a way that makes the reporter feel that he did the right thing by making the report.

Generally, someone interviews the reporter to gather the operative facts fully and in more detail than the initial report. When conducting this interview, you should:

- Determine who, what, where, when, why and how.
- Ask the reporter with whom do they think you should talk.
- Ask whom the reporter has spoken to about the issue.
- Ask what steps the reporter has taken to resolve or correct the issue.
- Ask whether the issue has affected the reporter's job in any way.
- Explore any surrounding circumstances, such as the relationship between the reporter and the subject, possible motives or bias.
- Request any relevant documents.
- Get as much detailed information as possible. A detailed first discussion helps to prepare a good, efficient investigation plan and reduces the number of times you may need to contact the reporter for more information.
- Not express opinions about the alleged conduct, and avoid opinions or comments about the character or ability of the others involved.
- Advise the reporter not to discuss the matter with others within the company except those with a need to know.
- Reassure the reporter that the company takes these reports seriously and will determine whether an investigation is needed. You should make clear that no final conclusion will be reached until the investigation has been completed.
- If the reporter asks whether he will receive a copy of a final report of the investigation, the reporter should be informed that although a final report will be prepared, they will not receive a copy.

Similarly, no specific, detailed report will be made to the reporter on management's response to the allegation.
- Advise the reporter to immediately report any actual or perceived retaliation for making the report.

Anonymous reports, however, should not be discounted unfairly. An anonymous report may be malicious or it may be valid and accurate. Remember that most employees do not trust management to keep their names confidential. Most people also do not want to be identified as the person responsible for bringing the matter to the attention of management. The detail provided in the anonymous report, or the lack of it, may either validate or invalidate the report.

Whether anonymous or not, please keep some pointers in mind. First, one should consider the source of the report. Some reporters are simply more credible than others. No reporter's allegations should be rejected out of hand, although issues of bias or self-interest must also be considered.

Second, consider the substance of the report. Is it an employee-specific allegation, such as a payroll issue, that does not have systemic implications to the business? Or does it appear to be a process failure that impacts a significant business practice issue? Is there a possible legal or criminal violation? Is it a violation of shared values? The substance of the report is a key factor in determining how we should allocate resources in the investigation.

Third, determine whether there is sufficient information to determine if the allegations should be investigated. Additional inquiries should be made if additional facts are needed, the person raising the issue cannot supply the relevant facts, or there is a need to review documents.

Fourth, consider the credibility of the accusation. Have we received complaints like this before? Has this reporter made accusations in the past that demonstrate a motive other than to redress the matter? Does the reporter support the allegations with specific facts that show personal knowledge or furnish documents proving his or her claims?

The Personal Interview

While documents may give you the clearest record of key events, the most revealing information comes from employees. The pivotal element of almost every workplace investigation is the employee interview.

Employees are sources of tremendous information. When they cooperate, they can explain relevant facts and interpret relevant documents. They can give insights into management styles and corporate cultures that put specific employee conduct into context.

Whom to Interview

Investigators generally interview every person who has possible knowledge of relevant facts. These would include, therefore, some or all of the following people:

- The reporter (if identified).
- The subject of the investigation.
- Anyone who observed a relevant incident.
- Other witnesses with relevant information, whether identified by the complaining employee or the subject.
- Authors of relevant documents.
- The supervisor of the subject.
- People whom the reporter has asked you to interview.
- People whom the subject has asked you to interview.

Interviews should focus on those with first-hand knowledge of the situation. you should resist the temptation to interview as many people as possible. you must keep the scope of the investigation as limited as possible.

Order of Interviews

Once you know who you want to interview, you then have to decide in what order to do it. Witnesses should then be interviewed in a logical fashion from the least likely to the most likely to be involved. Interviews can

As a general rule, documents should be examined before interviews begin. This will give you an understanding of the potential evidentiary value of the investigation, as well as to protect the security of documents. It will also allow you to understand the nature of the matters at issue, to identify key players, and to plan for interviews.

Interviews from witnesses to corroborate facts should be done after the neutral third-party witnesses. These witnesses may be cooperative or uncooperative. The focus of the interview should be to determine whether the witness observed the incidents in question, but do not limit the inquiry to only those incidents described by the complaining employee or the alleged offender. You should find our how the witness has been affected by observation of the incidents, and what he has done about it.

Those suspected of complicity should be interviewed next, from the least culpable to the most culpable. If appropriate, law enforcement could be contacted and involved in the process.

Generally, the subject of the investigation is interviewed last. There will be a natural tendency and irresistible impulse to confront and/or suspend those suspected of misconduct. However, this must be balanced against the extent to which critical fact-finding will be impeded at an early stage of the investigation. Pre-confrontation investigation will frequently uncover important facts reflecting the nature and extent of the misconduct, allowing the company to assess the harm. Facts which directly or circumstantially implicate the investigation subject may also be uncovered. This will enhance the likelihood that the later confrontation will be successful.

Even if it is believed that the subject will admit wrongdoing at the interview, an interview is still necessary. You should inform the subject individual's immediate supervisor of the report and your intention to interview the individual, requesting that the supervisor be vigilant for further problems, retaliation or other reactions which may affect the investigation. The subject should be given full information about the report against him and a full opportunity to explain and defend against the allegations. You should reinforce the fairness of the process by giving the subject every opportunity to explain his or her actions.

There is an exception to this interviewing order. In some circumstances, it may be best to conduct interviews without advance warning. Surprise interviews may be necessary when there is a concern that witnesses will alter or destroy evidence or that witnesses will confer with each other in an attempt to make their accounts consistent.

If all else fails, begin at the bottom and work up the chain of responsibility rather than begin at the top and work down. Productive sources can always be re-interviewed later.

Where to Conduct the Interview

The location of the interview should be a place that is conducive to effective information-gathering and protects the fairness of the process. You should pursue an interview as a business function and not as a criminal interrogation. It should be a relatively benign environment, and the witness should be physically free to get up and leave at any time. The room should be at normal temperature and should be free of distractions.

A comfortable setting encourages candid disclosures. Telephone interviews should be done as a last resort because the witness controls his or her setting, and you cannot observe the witness' body language or anything the witness is reading or doing. You may not even be aware that someone else may be monitoring the conversation.

Interviews in restaurants or other public places should be rarely used because there are too many distractions and risks to confidentiality. Off-site and home visits can be useful, however, when you seek to gain the witness' cooperation to further the investigation. Maintaining the secrecy of the interview enables the investigation to remain secret if the witness agrees to cooperate. An off-site location might also be chosen if there is any concern about violence or other disruption in the workplace as a result of confronting the witness.

You should also consider the psychological impact of an off-site confrontation. Confronting a subject at home, for example, can be effective if you are concerned that the witness may give false information to protect the company. A home confrontation conversely may backfire as it might offend the witness. You must balance the benefits and disadvantages.

Interview Dynamics

Every human interaction has interpersonal dynamics. In an interview, you must gain and continually control the discussion. If you do not control the witness, the witness will likely divert the interview process, leading the interview in directions the witness chooses. Worse, the witness can become you.

In an interview, control means the ability to get a witness to respond to your questioning. Response is the key element. The witness will always respond somehow. The critical issue is whether the witness will respond as you wish. Control over the interview is derived from your ability to persuade the witness to respond in the desired manner to your questions. An interview is neither an argument nor a debate.

You should never get angry. Becoming angry amounts to giving control of one's emotions to the witness, which is the opposite of the goal—to control the witness' emotions. If you cannot control your own emotions, you cannot control the witness. Whatever the subject of the investigation did, he did not do it to you personally. (And if the subject did, you should not be conducting the investigation.) You should recognize the investigation as a business problem that needs to be resolved in a business-like manner.

Giving Instructions to the Witness

It is likely that many or most of the employees you interview in an investigation will be nervous and understandably apprehensive. You should briefly explain at the start of the interview what is going on and what is expected of the witness. Consider these preliminary steps to create the right atmosphere:

- Please read the "Instructions for Witnesses" aloud to the witness.
- You may give the witness a brief explanation of the matter we are investigating. You may also explain why the witness has been included in the investigation (e.g., that they have been identified as someone with a complaint, have been accused of misconduct, or have been identified as someone who may have information relevant to the investigation). Reinforce your role as a fact-finder by asking for the witness' help in determining what happened.
- You should not stress any time limits on the interview. The witness should never be given the impression that there is a time limit on the meeting. Make the witness believe that the company is sufficiently concerned about the matter. Conversely, you should not accept unreasonable limits on their investigations that would interfere with their ability to conduct a professional interview.
- The witness may ask if he is being forced to submit to an interview. An employee should be free to leave at any time. Make it clear that the witness can leave or terminate the discussion at any time. Never force an employee to present himself against his will—either physically or through threats of termination—for an interview. However, an employer has the right to question employees regarding conduct connected with work, and to require cooperation as a condition of employment. If an employee does not wish to cooperate, they may refuse, but they may lose their job for refusing to cooperate. If the witness refuses to be interviewed, call the Investigations Manager for assistance.
- Employees often ask whether they are in trouble or whether they will be disciplined. The best answer is usually to be straightforward—it is certainly possible that employees may be disciplined if they engage in misconduct, but at this point in the investigation you are just gathering the facts. Never represent to a witness that

their cooperation may be offered as a quid pro quo for avoiding any disciplinary, civil or criminal action.
- A witness may ask if he needs a lawyer. You must offer no opinion on that. Management is not required to allow interview subjects to have a lawyer and can insist that the interview continue with the witness without a lawyer present. However, if the witness insists on having a lawyer present or he will refuse to be interviewed further, please stop the interview and call the Investigations Manager for further assistance
- A witness may ask if he may have a co-worker present during the interview. Generally, this should be discouraged. However, if a witness reasonably believes that the interview will result in disciplinary action against them, this may be allowed. The co-worker should be admonished not to interfere with the questioning or the answers offered by the witness. The co-worker cannot play any role in the interview. The co-worker should not be someone who may have some connection—especially as a witness—to the matter you are investigating.
- Please be sure that your witness is speaking from personal knowledge. If he is relying on some information that they, in turn, learned from someone else, please note that as well as the identity of that other person.
- You should invite the witness to give a written personal statement of the relevant facts if the witness wishes to do so. (This is contained in the witness instructions, and a template form is attached to this guide.) The statement should contain a record of the issues raised, the witness' version of what happened, who was involved, witnesses, dates, etc. The statement should also respond to or explain any evidence. The reason to offer this is because questions necessarily reflect those matters about which you wish to get information. The witness statement, by contrast, reflects what the witness wants to say about the matter. The written statement may give you additional information about the investigation. Additionally, the offer to the witness reinforces the fairness of the investigation process by allowing them to present their views. The written statement should be signed, dated and added to the file. Please remind the witness, however, that this is not substitute for the interview.

Asking the Best Questions in the Interview

You now have your witness, the place for the interview, and all the preliminaries are done. You are ready to begin.

Witness interviews as part of a workplace investigation are neither pretrial depositions nor cross-examinations at trial. The purpose of the interview is simply to elicit truthful, relevant information. You should phrase your questions and ask them in a manner designed to achieve that purpose. For a productive interview, please keep the following points in mind:

- Remember the 80:20 rule. You are there to acquire knowledge, not disclose it. Generally, the witness should be talking 80% of the time, and you only approximately 20% of the time.
- The interview should center on the specific misconduct at which the investigation is aimed. Transforming the interview into a wide-ranging inquisition into all possible areas of misconduct is counterproductive because it detracts from the focus of the investigation.
- The initial discovery of what appeared to be isolated misconduct may be just a symptom of a much larger problem. You should keep alert to that possibility.
- Sometimes, managers may want to participate in, or attend, interviews of various witnesses. This can have a chilling effect on the witness. Generally, it is best to conduct the interviews of employees without their managers present.
- You should use a non-confrontational approach. A witness is more likely to cooperate with someone he likes, or at least feel reasonably comfortable with, rather than someone he considers threatening. There may be times when it is necessary to take a more harsh approach. Nonetheless, in the first instance, it is almost always beneficial to try a more disarming approach.
- You should ask questions in chronological or other systematic order, not randomly. If questioning is confusing, you will lose the witness's train of thought and risk missing information.
- You should not expect the witness to have an exact recollection of events that occurred some time ago. Even honest people don't remember everything. It is your obligation to refresh the witness' recollection with documents or other information, if needed.
- There are no "magic questions" to ask when interviewing someone. But you will never fail if you asks the "who, what, where, when, why and how" questions.

- However, you should avoid asking "why" questions until the end. These questions are usually antagonistic because they sound moralistic.
- You should ask open-ended questions. Open-ended questions are more likely to result in your learning what the witness knows. "Who was there?" "What was said?" "Why did you do that?" Open-ended questions encourage the witness to respond. They allow you to learn about the subject, based on how the witness describes himself. They help the witness relax.
- You should not ask close-ended questions. This type of question tends to require a "yes" or "no," or a brief statement at most. These questions do not provide for extended responses and, as a rule, do not cause the witness to relax. The witness is more likely to provide the answer and then stop talking.
- You should ask straightforward questions. You should not be cute, tricky or shrewd.
- The basis of the witness' knowledge is always important. You must determine whether the witness is speaking from personal knowledge or just relying on the hearsay statements of others. "How do you know that?" is a question to ask often.
- You should ask the witness to list all individuals who have knowledge of any of the events. "Who else might know?" is a question to ask often.
- You should ask short, simple questions. You are more likely to get clear, responsive answers by asking understandable questions.
- You should distinguish between words used by the witness and situations where the witness simply agrees with a question or statement. You should consider the wording of leading questions and whose words were used. You should identify situations where there were only agreements with statements made by you or the witness made the actual statements.
- The investigation should identify any mitigating circumstances that may affect the assessment of fault, such as personal or health problems.
- It may not always be possible, but you should try to structure questions which do not call attention to particular problem areas. The order of questions as well as your demeanor in asking them can alert a witness to the focus and severity of the problem being investigation. If there is something you would prefer to remain

highly confidential, you should take care in structuring and asking the questions to the witness. (Some questioners even include subjects of no real relevance to avoid tipping the witness to the nature of the inquiry.)
- You should save unfriendly or embarrassing questions until the end of the interview. Beginning with the "tough" questions may cause the witness to become defensive.
- On key factual questions it can be valuable to return to the same question more than once in different ways. People often remember things in waves, and this approach may develop additional detail.
- If a person does not remember, you should try to help by asking questions that help recreate the situation when the event occurred, but do not suggest an answer.
- Silence is a great technique. Many people cannot stand silence and find this unnerving. They will fill up the void with talk, often saying something they had no intention of revealing. The average person expects no more than seven seconds of silence during a conversation. If you don't say anything after the witness answers a question, the witness will frequently give you more information than he intended to give you. The silence effectively pressured the subject into offering more information by communicating that you felt that the answer was not complete. Silence can also be an effective way to undermine a witness who is cocky and confident in his or her own ability to control the discussion. The witness, and not you, should become uncomfortable with the silence.
- You should avoid doing anything that might be taken as an attempt to influence the witness' answers. You should avoid characterizing the company's position, summarizing the statements of other witnesses, or selectively presenting documents in a way that may distort the facts.
- There is always the possibility that the information the witness is providing contradicts either something they said earlier or a piece of information gathered from another source. One of the most effective techniques is to note the contradictions and than, at the appropriate point, ask the witness how these contradictory facts could be true (or reconciled). You may recall them individually and review the facts again.
- You should ask again at the end of the interview: "Is there anything else relevant to this matter that I should know? Is there anything I

missed? What else should I ask you? What other documents are important? Who else knows about this? Who else can help me with this information? Is there a question I should have asked and didn't? Is there anything else you know about this?" Ask several of these questions. It is very important to document these questions to support the fact that the witness was asked for all relevant information.

Listening and Observing in an Interview

Actively listen. You must work very hard at listening. It is much more than concentrating. You must also be thinking about what the person is telling you. Is what he is telling you logical? Does it make sense? Is there a "backstory" to explain what happened?

Show interest in what the speaker has to say. Ask questions to clarify, gather information and focus the conversation.

Carefully observe the witness's body posture and physical activity. Everyone uses body language to express themselves. Watch for changes in appearance in response to certain questions. Most people under stress are unaware of their reactions. Use your observations to aid in formulating questions.

Gather information to assess the witness' credibility. How did the witness react to the allegations? Does the person inspire confidence in the listener? Does the witness' chronology of the relevant events differ greatly from those of others? Was the witness forthcoming with information?

Closing the Interview

At the end of the interview, you should thank the witness for the information furnished. You should give the witness your telephone number if more information becomes available or is remembered. You should keep the door open for future contact if they would like to add or change anything. The goal is to obtain the most accurate information possible. An interview is not intended to be a memory test.

If you asked the witness to furnish documents, this is the time to renew that request and agree to a list and date for production, if possible, of the needed documents. You should consider giving the witness a written list of the items he has to furnish. You should follow up a few days later to confirm the request.

You should tell the witness that appropriate management personnel will make any final determination regarding the best way to resolve the issue, but you should stress that that the witness' input is valuable and will be considered seriously. The witness should be told that the results of the investigation remain confidential and that the specific corrective actions may not be communicated to the witness.

The interview does not need to have covered all the facts, events and conduct. All you need to move forward are the basic elements of the conduct alleged.

Collection and Review of Documents

Witnesses may be reluctant to supply information voluntarily, especially when it may implicate their own actions or the actions of those they supervise or with whom they work. Similarly, witness recollections of events often fade with time and may be inconsistent with recollections of other witnesses. Documents are essential in the process of refreshing a witness' memory and might also help you reconcile conflicting recollections. Documents can also help determine or assess a person's intent or motive in doing something.

Please take certain precautions when handling documents in an investigation. Original documents should not be marked or altered in any way. An original document is any document that is received by you, even if it is a copy. It does not include any copies made by you. If you need a working copy of the document, please copy the original. Put the original in your file, and mark the copies up as needed. Following this practice will prevent an inadvertent alteration of original documents and ensure that these documents will not be invalidated or challenged later as a result of your markings.

The authenticity of documents may become very important in cases where document tampering is suspected. Therefore, in some instances it may become necessary to obtain the same documents from more than one independent source. Be sure to indicate which copy of the document came from which source.

III. Reporting your Results

Interview Memos

What a witness says in an interview is critical to the investigation. An accurate written record of what they say is key to the integrity of the investigation, the success of the investigation, and the fairness to those involved.

You should draft a memorandum shortly after the interview. The interview memo must represent exactly what went on in the interview in detail. If the interview took an hour, the hour must be accounted for on paper. The interview memo simply cannot be three lines long. Include everything that was said and done. Please keep the following points in mind:

- The interview memo must be factual and should not contain your opinions. Don't say, for example, that "John Smith appeared uninterested." Say (only if it is accurate), "John Smith continually looked around the room and requested that questions be repeated to him two or three times before he would answer."
- Use direct quotes whenever possible. They strengthen the factual assertions.
- When possible, refer to relevant company policies, practices and written procedures. If possible, reach findings that are supported directly by the information you gathered.
- Avoid expressing opinions because opinions can easily be challenged. Once doubt is brought to opinions expressed in the interview memo, the credibility of the interview memo, report and investigation may also be challenged. It is better to focus on what the facts show, rather than what you personally conclude from your inquiries.
- Avoid inflammatory or judgmental words. The interview is intended to gather facts only, not pass judgments on others. Also, write your interview memo as if your report will be published. It might be included in documents that are more widely circulated.
- If you want to make an assertion about some aspect of your inquiries, please support it with the facts you gathered. Our goal is only to determine whether the report can be substantiated.
- Do not make legal conclusions about any perceived law violations, breaches of contract, or potential corporate liability. These conclusions would be outside the scope of the investigation.
- The interview memo should also include any contradictions surfaced during the interview. Contradictions can exist between documents and interviews, among different witnesses or when the witness contradicts himself. Please indicate whether, through your efforts, you were able to resolve any conflicts in testimony or documents.
- If any documents were used, be sure to mention them, whether or not their use resulted in any response from the witness such as an admission. Their use demonstrates how diligently you attempted to

get the truth and how professionally they conducted themselves. In a particular case, for example, they could show how, in spite of all the proof, the witness denied the act or contradicted himself, herself, others or documents. If a document was used, mention that fact.
- If an acknowledgement, admission or confession is made, be specific as to exactly what was admitted. If the individual acknowledged doing two things, write out exactly what happened so that a reader cannot possibly incorrectly believe that he admitted to doing ten or only one.
- Record any other significant events that occurred during the interview, such as the witness began to cry, or shouted, or refused to speak any further.
- Be brief, but please tell a complete story. Write for an educated audience, but not someone who is knowledgeable about your business.
- Handwritten notes taken by a questioner during an interview are very subjective and often written in shorthand form. As a result, the true interpretation of the notes may be known only to the questioner and could be subject to a variety of interpretations by other readers. Therefore, once you have written your interview memo, discard your notes. A complete, strictly accurate interview memo should be the only documentation of the interview.

The Final Report

Your work may lead to the creation of a second type of document, the Final Report. The Final Report is created at the conclusion of the investigation and includes the report and a summary of the facts gathered throughout the investigation.

Written reports can be valuable aids for management to develop corrective procedures to avoid repetitions of questionable conduct. A written report may also be a persuasive way of communicating to third parties that wrongful conduct did not occur or that corrective action has been taken internally. The report also forces us to reach firm conclusions and is an easy way to review the results of the investigation with executive management.

The quality of the Final Report depends almost entirely on your efforts. The Final Report is not a chronology of the investigation. The report states whether the report was substantiated, unsubstantiated, or that the findings were inconclusive. If the report is substantiated, the Final Report will cite the policies violated and the harm the company suffered as a result. If the employee admits wrongdoing or resigns before the Final Report is issued, the report will include that information as well.

The Final Report is limited to the scope of the investigation. The scope will be clearly specified in the report. This will provide a clear understanding to anyone to whom the report is disclosed regarding the investigation's limitations.

Once all the questions are addressed and the investigation is concluded, the Final Report is prepared. The report includes:

- The nature of the report and how it brought to our attention;
- A summary of the facts gathered throughout the investigation, including a chronology of events,
- The people interviewed and the documents reviewed;
- A brief discussion of any credibility assessments reached;
- Whether the report was substantiated or unsubstantiated or the results were inconclusive. If substantiated, what conclusions are supported by what was found;
- The specific conclusion(s) reached on each key issue;
- The identification of any issues that could not be resolved in the investigation;
- A brief discussion of how the company guidelines or policies apply to the situation;
- Whether a breakdown in an internal control occurred to allow the claimed problem to occur;
- Whether any relevant internal controls were followed to prevent other problems or reduce the impact;
- For what period did the problem occurred, and what, if any, is the financial impact to The Company or third parties;
- How is The Company responding to the report, if it is substantiated; and
- A list of the documents gathered for the investigation.

The Final Report offers no recommendations regarding how an employee should be disciplined, whether the Company should compensate someone, or similar post-investigation activity. Those steps are outside the scope of the investigation. However, if the appropriate business unit makes such a determination before the Final Report is drafted, that information is included as part of the facts of the investigation.

APPENDIX K

Memo

To: John Smith
From:
Date: January 1, 2007
Subject: Internal Investigation—Case #000
Chicago, Illinois

    I write to confirm our telephone conversation. As I told you, an allegation has been raised that we would like to discuss with you. We have already gathered some preliminary information regarding the situation, and we would like to speak to you because we believe you have information that is relevant to the matters under investigation. I cannot share details concerning the matter today and ask you not to discuss our conversation with anyone in the company.
    I would like to meet with you as soon as possible. Would you be available to meet with me in your office at 9:00 on January 9th?
    The purpose of this meeting is to gather information regarding the issue and your role in the situation. I will be asking you specific questions regarding your recollections and observations. I will also ask you for any documents you have that may be relevant to the investigation.
    Your honesty, truthfulness, and confidentiality are critical to resolve this situation as soon as possible. Please know that, regardless of the allegation, no one is presumed to have acted improperly, unethically or in violation of company rules unless the investigation proves otherwise. No conclusions will be made until all the facts have been reviewed.
    Please feel free to contact me at (___) ___-____ with any questions.

APPENDIX L

Memo

To: John Smith
From:
Date: January 1, 2007
Subject: Internal Investigation—Case #000
Chicago, Illinois

    I write to confirm our telephone conversation. As I told you, an allegation has been raised that we would like to discuss with you. We have already gathered some preliminary information regarding the situation, and we would like to speak to you because we believe you have information that is relevant to the matters under investigation. Please know that the allegation involves you personally.

    I would like to meet with you as soon as possible. Would you be available to meet with me in your office at 9:00 on January 9th?

    The purpose of this meeting is to gather information regarding the issue and your role in the situation. I will be asking you specific questions regarding your recollections and observations. I will also ask you for any documents you have that may be relevant to the investigation.

    Because the allegation involves you personally, we want to give you the opportunity to confirm or deny certain of the facts we have uncovered. We also want to allow you to give us your account of these events. This interview may be your best opportunity to explain your role in the matters under review.

    Your honesty, truthfulness, and confidentiality are critical to resolve this situation as soon as possible. Please know that, regardless of the allegation, no one is presumed to have acted improperly, unethically or in violation of company rules unless the investigation proves otherwise. No conclusions will be made until all the facts have been reviewed.

    Please feel free to contact me at (___) ___-____ with any questions.

APPENDIX M

Instructions for Witnesses

This is a workplace investigation. It is a serious matter. You have been asked to assist us. We are trying to find out what happened here so we can advise management accordingly. We appreciate your time and cooperation.

I will not mislead you or lie to you. You should not lie to me. Lying in the course of the investigation can get you in serious trouble.

If you are an attorney, add: Please know that I am a lawyer. I represent the company, and I do not represent the investigator. Anything we discuss here today is not subject to the attorney-client privilege, and I may share this information with company management.

You should cooperate fully, with complete candor, and respond to all questions and requests honestly. If you do not understand a question, please let me know, and I will clarify it. If you do not ask for a clarification, I will assume the investigator understood the question.

I am interested in what the investigator know based on your own personal knowledge. Please do not speculate. If you do not know the answer to a question, please say so. Don't guess.

We presume that anyone subject of acting illegally, unethically, or in violation of company policy is innocent until the investigation proves otherwise. We will make no conclusions until all the facts have been reviewed.

Investigations are conducted confidentially. Do not discuss this investigation with anyone, unless I tell the investigator otherwise. Information is disclosed internally only on a need-to-know basis.

We will not tolerate any type of threat or retaliation against anyone who reports a violation or cooperates in an investigation. If you receive any such threats, please advise me immediately. I will give you my business card.

Do not ask me who reported a violation or who else may be cooperating in the investigation. We want to protect the reputation of anyone involved in the investigation, and you do not necessarily know the full scope of our inquiries.

Do not play detective. Do not draw any conclusions as a result of this interview. This interview is only part of the investigation.

Please keep all records relating to the investigation. Don't destroy anything.

My goal is to obtain the best information possible. If the investigator later remember anything that the investigator couldn't remember here today, or the investigator want to supplement or correct something the investigator said, please call me. I would be happy to make the necessary changes.

If you want, you may give me a written statement concerning the matters we are discussing. This is entirely voluntary. you have no obligation to do so. However, this will give the investigator the chance to explain the facts as the investigator believe them to be. I have the form for your use if you choose to make such a statement. I will then add it to the investigations file.

APPENDIX N

Personal Statement

Your details:
Name:
Title:
Office Location:
Phone:

Your statement (attach additional sheets to this page if needed):

This statement is true to the best of my knowledge and belief. I understand that I will be subject to company discipline if I have wilfully stated anything that I know to be false or do not believe to be true.

Signed: _____ Date: _____

APPENDIX O

Final Investigation Report

Case Number:
Business Unit:
Location:
Investigator:
Report Date

This final report is prepared in connection with the investigation. The report is based on supporting documents provided in the course of the investigation, an understanding of the relevant facts and on information collected during the course of the investigation.

The investigation has been limited solely to a determination of the relevant facts. No opinion is offered regarding the findings, possible disciplinary decisions, or considerations of potential legal liability.

1 Investigation location
The company business unit is _____. The company office is located at _____.

2 The report
The misconduct allegations investigated were:

The investigation determined that the allegations of misconduct are: (substantiated or unsubstantiated).

3 Investigative steps
The investigation sought to establish whether the allegations could be proven by the available facts and, regardless of the outcome, the various policy and process improvements that could be improved.

Interviews were taken as part of the investigation. Interviews were taken of each of the following employees:

The key documents reviewed were:

4 Findings on the allegation

Summary of findings: The allegation was (substantiated or unsubstantiated). Specifically:

Specific factual findings:

5 Post-investigation information

6 Evaluation of business processes and internal controls

APPENDIX P

Memo

To: Department Employees
From:
Date: January 1, 2007
Subject: Reminder of Policy against Retaliation

As you know, we recently concluded an investigation involving one or more people in your department. Out of an abundance of caution, we wanted to remind each of you that the company prohibits you from retaliating against anyone who lodged a complaint against a co-worker—whether it has merit or not—or cooperated with the investigation.

It is human nature for a person who was the subject of an investigation or who had to submit to an interview to have hard feelings or believe that others may have been causing problems for the company. When people begin to act on those feelings in a negative way, they may be engaging in conduct that could be viewed as retaliation.

Although there is no complete list, acts of retaliation include each of the following:

- Discussing or gossiping about the report or a witness' participation in the investigation.
- Openly laughing at or referring to the employee in a harsh or derogatory way.
- Ignoring or avoiding the employee in an obvious mannner
- Failing to provide the employee with critical information needed to perform his job or ensure his personal safety in the workplace.
- Blaming the employee for causing a problem because the employee filed a complaint.
- Remarking that the employee should transfer to another department or quit their job.
- Threatening or harassing the employee.

Because the investigation is complete, the company now considers the matter closed. The company will take whatever actions, if any, that it deems appropriate. There is no valid business reason for continuing to address these matters, and we appreciate your cooperation as we move forward.

APPENDIX Q

Business Ethics Bulletin #1

As part of our commitment to an ethical workplace and to ensure that the company meets its legal obligations, the Company requires colleagues and associates to report possible violations of the Code of Business Conduct. The company responds to these reports. From time to time, the lessons learned from an investigation are relevant to the operations of other business groups. We would like to inform you about the results of a recent investigation which may be of interest to you.

Incident

After a routine audit, a client alleged that they were fraudulently overbilled for services. Compliance investigated the matter and determined that the Company's job-site supervisor (the "Supervisor") at the client's location falsified timecards and then kept the over-payment. The Supervisor refused to cooperate with the investigation and was terminated. Law-enforcement authorities were also contacted.

The Supervisor had near-total management control over the workers at the site. The local district office's internal processes allowed the Supervisor—without the involvement of anyone else—to (ii) to put a job listing in the system; (ii) assign a worker to fill that listing; (iii) handle the time cards; (iv) calculate the invoice and instruct the district office to send the invoice to the client; (v) have checks delivered to the district office; and (vi) retrieve those checks from the district office and distribute them to the associates.

When weekly payroll checks were generated for the associates, the check would be directed to the district office if that associate had not arranged for direct deposit. The normal practice was for the Supervisor to retrieve the checks from the district office and distribute them to the associates. Of course, if an associate did not work that week and the timecard was fabricated, the Supervisor took the check, cashed it at a check-cashing service that participated in the scheme, and kept the money.

Key Takeaways

Cause of Incident: Procedures placed too much authority solely with the Supervisor. This was compounded by allowing the Supervisor to handle timecards, obtain associate paychecks and distribute these checks without the participation of others. The fraud would likely not have happened if another colleague had been involved in the process.

Managers who are responsible for on-site supervisors should examine their own procedures to ensure that sufficient controls are in place to prevent such a fraud from occurring.

Policy Violated: The Code of Conduct states that: "All employees are required to understand and abide by internal financial control procedures relating to their job functions [including] . . . . complete and accurate entries on time sheets and expense reports" and "accurate record keeping."

Falsification of billing records and fraud is serious misconduct and a business-ethics violation that will result in severe disciplinary action, up to and including termination.

The monetary value related to an ethics violation does not mitigate the severity of the offense or the resulting disciplinary action.

Escalation Process: Any colleague or associate should immediately report any suspected ethics or compliance-related violation to their Supervisor or Human Resources, or call the Ethics hotline. The hotline accepts anonymous calls. Company policy forbids retaliation against any employee who comes forward with a good-faith complaint of inappropriate conduct.

Additional Resources: The Code of Conduct is available externally at _____. For further training and guidance on business conduct and ethics, visit *www._____.com.*

Release Date:
Contact for Additional Information:

APPENDIX R

Memo

To: John Smith
From:
Date: January 1, 2007
Subject: Internal Investigation—Case #000
                    Thank You and Follow Up

    We write regarding the information you recently provided to the company regarding a possible violation of ethics rules or company procedures. This note is to inform you that we have just recently completed our workplace investigation.

    We appreciate your cooperation during this process. Your involvement has been important to the company's commitment to maintaining the highest standards of ethical conduct and business integrity.

    Although the details of our investigation are confidential, the findings have been shared with the relevant members of management. If appropriate, corrective steps will be taken to address the matter.

    Please feel free to contact me at (___) ___-____ with any questions. Thank you again for your assistance.

Made in the USA
San Bernardino, CA
23 August 2015